GREAT WALKS

NORTH WALES

FRANK DUERDEN
Photography by John Heseltine

This special edition has been
produced in 1992
by New Orchard Editions Ltd,
Villiers House, 41/47 Strand,
London WC2N 5JE,
a Cassell company
for publication
by Printwise Publications Ltd,
47 Bradshaw Road, Tottington,
Bury, Lancs, BL8 3PW

Reprinted 1994

Maps based upon the Ordnance Survey map
with the sanction of the Controller of Her
Majesty's Stationery Office.

Designed by Niki fforde

Printed and bound in Spain by Graficromo S.A.

ISBN 1 872226 58 2

Contents

Acknowledgments 6
Introduction 7

The Snowdonia National Park (Parc Cenedlaethol Eryri) 9

THE FACE OF SNOWDONIA 12

Drystone walls 12
The Forestry Commission 13
Hafod and hendref 14
The Ice Age in North Wales 15
The Nature Conservancy Council 15
Rock climbing 16
Search and Rescue helicopters in Snowdonia 17
The sheep dog 18
Sheep farming 19
Signposts and stiles 20
Slate 20
The Welsh Black 22
The Welsh language 22
Wild goats 22

Selected Walks in the Snowdonia National Park 23

Introduction to the route descriptions 24

1. EASY ROUTES

1. The Torrent Walk 28
2. Through the Llugwy Gorge 30
3. The Precipice Walk 34
4. To the Rhaeadr-fawr, the Aber Falls 38
5. Through the Gwydyr Forest 42
6. The Roman Steps 46
7. Cwm Bychan and the Pass of Aberglaslyn 49
8. Cwm Idwal and the Devil's Kitchen 57

2. MODERATE ROUTES

9. Conwy Mountain and the Sychnant Pass 62
10. The Pony Track to Penygadair (Northern Route) 68
11. The Ascent of Rhinog Fawr 71
12. The Ascent of Moel Hebog 75
13. The Traverse of the Glyder Ridge 80
14. The Ascent of Moel Siabod 88
15. The Traverse of Cader Idris 95
16. The Eastern Carneddau 100
17. The Central Rhinogydd 108
18. The Ascent of Cnicht 114
19. The Traverse of Snowdon 120

3. MORE STRENUOUS ROUTES

20. The Nantlle Ridge 129
21. The Southern Rhinogydd 135
22. The Nant Ffrancon Ridge, Y Garn to Elidir Fawr 142
23. Carnedd Llewelyn from Ogwen 149
24. The Snowdon Horseshoe 159
25. The Idwal Skyline 168
26. The Great Ridge of the Carneddau 172

4. VERY STRENUOUS ROUTES

27. The Welsh 1000 metres 178
28. The Welsh Three Thousands 182

APPENDICES

Access for the walker 186
Safety 187
Giving a grid reference 188
Countryside Access Charter 189
Addresses of useful organizations 190

Index 192

Acknowledgments

I must acknowledge the considerable help given to me during the preparation of *Great Walks of North Wales* by many people, most of whom are involved one way or another in the life of North Wales.

In particular, I must thank John Ellis Roberts, now Head Warden of the northern area of the Snowdonia National Park; John Fox, warden of the Christian Adventure Trust Hostel at Rhyd-ddu; and Fred Taylor, host of the Llugwy Guest House at Capel Curig until his death in 1982, who looked over my preliminary list of walks and made many useful suggestions.

The late Mr Hywel Roberts (National Park Officer 1974–82), Mr Alan Jones (National Park Officer), Mr D. Archer, Miss M. Rees and Mr P. A. Ogden of the Snowdonia National Park Authority supplied me with a great deal of information as did officials of the Forestry Commission at Aberystwyth, the Nature Conservancy Council at Ffordd Penrhos, and the National Trust at Llandudno. Mr R. J. Jones of the North Western Region of the Central Electricity Generating Board at Stockport provided information on their power stations at Trawsfynydd, Cwm Dyli and Dinorwic; the Snowdon Mountain Railway Company on the railway and summit hotel; and Flight Lieutenant A. J. Magson, WRAF, of RAF Valley on aircraft and rescue helicopters in Snowdonia. Mr John Keylock (Publicity Manager and Director of the Welsh Highland Light Railway Company) helped me with the sections on the railway and Mr Dan Jones (County Secretary of The National Farmers' Union at Caernarfon) read through the sections on farming and The Welsh Black. Dr Y. Williams of The Polytechnic of North London gave me advice with the sections on geology; Mr Brian Williams and Mr John Stoddard with the pronunciation and the English meaning of Welsh words; Mr C. B. Briggs with the history of Pen-y-Gwryd and Mr Glyn Jones with the section on sheep-dogs. Messrs H. Nicholls and P. Abnett explored one small section of a route for me.

I must thank the following for permission to use material from their publications: Wm Collins Sons and Co. Ltd (extracts from *Wild Wales* by George Borrow; the Countryside Commission (The Countryside Access Charter); the Ordnance Survey (list of maps and details of mountains); the Snowdonia National Park Authority (extracts from the Snowdonia National Park Plan, 1977) and Gwynedd County Council Planning Department (Gwynedd Tourism Survey, 1980). The maps were drawn from the Outdoor Leisure maps with the permission of the Ordnance Survey.

Finally, I must thank Miss Jacqueline Montague, Miss Patricia Webster, Mrs Jennifer Peck and my daughter, Sharon, who typed the manuscripts and my wife, Audrey, and daughter, Beverley, who helped me with the proofreading.

Introduction

My first acquaintance with the mountains of Snowdonia was through the pages of *Let's Go Climbing* by Colin Kirkus. Kirkus was one of the best British climbers in the period between the two world wars, who made his name mainly in North Wales. His book, which I found very inspiring, was my walking and climbing 'bible' for many of my early years. Therefore, by the time that I paid my first visit to the mountains of Snowdonia in 1949, and made my first — and compulsory — ascent of Yr Wyddfa, I felt that I already knew them very well. Many visits and numerous ascents later, I am rather less confident, but the years have certainly not wearied me of them. Quite the opposite. Moel Siabod, Cnicht, Yr Wyddfa and Penyrole-wen are now old friends of mine.

The walks described here are, in my opinion, the finest within the Snowdonia National Park. They cover — quite deliberately — a very wide range both of length and of difficulty, so as to appeal to as many walkers as possible; although obviously, because of the nature of the terrain, mountain walks tend to predominate. Each route description is accompanied by an account of the main features of interest along the way, because while Snowdonia is a popular holiday area, it is also the work-place for some 27,000 people and has a rich cultural and historical heritage. It was thought that the walks would become more interesting if the reader knew something of it. More general accounts which apply to the area as a whole, such as those on drystone walls, farming and the industry of North Wales, are brought together at the beginning under 'The face of Snowdonia'.

I would like to congratulate John Heseltine on his fine photographs which capture so magnificently the beauty and the magic of Snowdonia. They will, I am certain, help to brighten many a winter evening when I am well away from the hills.

The walks described here will take you into magnificent countryside, whether you are content to follow some of the easier ones along the valleys or wish to try some of the more ambitious routes up into the mountains. For the latter, particularly, perhaps a word of warning is not out of place. Unfortunately, each year, within the National Park, there are accidents and occasional deaths involving walkers. For this reason, a section on safety has been included, although, in the end, safety precautions must be left to the judgment of the individual concerned. Edward Whymper, well-known for his part in the first ascent of the Matterhorn in 1865, summed it up well: 'Climb if you will, but remember that courage and strength are naught without prudence, and that a momentary negligence may destroy the happiness of a lifetime. Do nothing in haste; look well to each step; and from the beginning think what may be the end . . .'

That is not to say, however, that you should be a mere 'fine-weather walker'. The walking days which tend to come most quickly back to my mind are usually those done in bad weather, with the rain coming down 'straight as stair rods' and the tops shrouded in mist. Probably, I suppose, because these expeditions represented much more of a challenge, even though the others may have seemed more enjoyable at the time. In any case, even the most unpromising of mornings can sometimes lead on to a superb day as the bad weather clears. On 25 August 1972 I climbed Snowdon along the Pyg Track. From Pen-y-Pass to Bwlch y Moch and the zig-zags I was in dense mist; then suddenly this cleared away and the whole summit was bathed in warm sunshine. From horizon to horizon the cloud sea was unbroken except where here and there some of the higher peaks of Snowdonia managed to break through as isolated islands.

Finally, it should be remembered that the world does not stand still. The information given, as far as is known, was accurate when collected, but inevitably time will erode its value. Fortunately, the route descriptions are likely to remain reasonably accurate for a long while as footpaths, field boundaries, woods, etc., in mountain areas do not change much. Where footpaths do change, it is usually as the result of a deliberate diversion, for example to allow a badly eroded path to recover, and the diversion will usually be well marked. In such cases, of course, the diversion should always be followed.

Frank Duerden

The Snowdonia National Park *(Parc Cenedlaethol Eryri)*

John Dower defined a National Park as 'an extensive area of beautiful and relatively wild country in which, for the nation's benefit and by appropriate national decision and action, (a) the characteristic landscape beauty is strictly preserved, (b) access and facilities for public open-air enjoyment are amply provided, (c) wild life and buildings and places of architectural and historic interest are suitably protected, while (d) established farming use is effectively maintained'.

The United Kingdom lagged behind many other countries of the world in the establishment of its National Parks. Argentina, Canada, Germany, Italy, New Zealand, Poland, South Africa, Spain, Sweden, Switzerland and the United States were among the countries which had National Parks before any were designated here.

Under the National Parks and Access to the Countryside Act of 1949 a National Parks Commission was established, which was responsible for the creation of National Parks; ten were created by the Commission in England and Wales between 1950 and 1957. In 1968 the National Parks Commission was replaced by the Countryside Commission, which therefore took over responsibility for the Parks. A further change came under the Local Government Act of 1972; under this Act a separate National Park Authority was set up for each National Park, charged with its administration. Each Authority was given the task of producing a National Park Plan by 1 April 1977, and of reviewing that plan at intervals of not more than five years. This set out the policies of the Authority for the management of its Park and proposals for carrying out those policies.

The National Park Authorities are charged with two main aims. The first is to preserve and enhance the natural beauty of the areas designated as National Parks, and the second to encourage the provision or improvement of facilities for the enjoyment of open-air recreation and the study of nature within the National Parks. They must in addition have due regard for the social and economic needs of the people living within the Parks.

The overall management of the Snowdonia National Park is

the responsibility of the Snowdonia National Park Committee within Gwynedd County Council. This has twenty-seven members nominated by Gwynedd County Council, the local District Councils and the Secretary of State for Wales (in the latter case after consultation with the Countryside Commission). The Committee is served by a number of sub-committees specially concerned with particular areas, interests such as farming and forestry, and special projects. A staff of full-time workers, under the overall control of the National Park Officer, are responsible for implementing the decisions of the Park Committee.

The National Park Authority receives the majority of its revenue from the Welsh Office (via the Countryside Commission) and Gwynedd County Council.

Some Facts and Figures about the Snowdonia National Park

DESIGNATED 1951. The Park was the third to be designated, after the Peak District and the Lake District National Parks.

AREA 838 sq miles (217,100 hectares). It is the second largest as the Lake District National Park occupies 866 sq miles (224,293 hectares).

LAND OWNERSHIP IN 1980 (%)

Private land 69.5	Welsh National Water Development Authority 0.9
Forestry Commission 15.6	Nature Conservancy Council 0.4
National Trust 8.8	National Park Authority 0.3
Secretary of State 3.3	Ministry of Defence 0.1
Central Electricity Generating Board 1.1	Total of 'public' land 30.5

RESIDENTS On the basis of census data the resident population of the Park in 1971 was estimated as 26,272. It has probably declined since then. The population of the Park tends to be rather older than that of England and Wales generally. 23.1% of males and 20.4% of females were fourteen years or younger, compared to the national averages of 25.1% and 22.5% respectively. 15.6% of males and 29.4% of females were sixty-five years or older, compared to 10.5% and 22% respectively.

TOURISTS A roadside survey in 1980 of people leaving the Park indicated that on a typical August day about 180,000 visitors who are staying in Gwynedd overnight visit the Park; there are in addition about 37,000 day visitors, i.e., who are not staying locally.

WHERE TOURISTS STAY (% 1980, GWYNEDD) The main categories are:

Rented chalets, cottages, etc. 15.1	Static caravans (rented) 10.2
	Friends and relatives 9.0

Second homes 5.5	Hotels, guest houses 10.7
Static caravans (owned) 14.7	Bed and breakfasts 4.4
Tents 13.5	Holiday camp 2.3

WHERE VISITORS COME FROM (% 1980, GWYNEDD)

The main categories are:

	Day visitors	*Staying visitors*
North Wales (excluding Gwynedd)	26	–
North-west	20	23
West Midlands	17	19
Merseyside	17	10
Mid-Wales	8	–
Greater Manchester	5	7
Birmingham	2	4
North-east	2	–
East Midlands	–	9
South-east	–	3

The Face of Snowdonia

Drystone Walls

As in many other mountain and moorland areas, stone walls are a conspicuous feature of the landscape of North Wales, separating low field from ffridd, ffridd from mountain and a farm from its neighbour. They run along and across the valleys, boldly ascend steep mountain sides and mark the line of ridges and of summits. Most of them were built in the eighteenth and nineteenth centuries, when throughout England and Wales vast areas of land were being enclosed. They are called drystone walls, because they were built entirely without mortar, their strength and durability products only of the skill and craft of the men who built them.

Stone was plentiful and near-to-hand in most areas of North Wales, but as approximately one ton was needed for each square yard of wall, the work was hard and called for judgment to avoid unnecessary labour. A waller would usually work with an assistant, one to each side of the wall, with their material stacked nearby. It was essentially a job for the warmer months of the year, for cold winds, driving rain and snow made the work too difficult at other times.

The lines of the wall would be marked out with pegs and string and wherever possible a trench cut to receive a level and firm foundation of large and heavy stones. Upon this the wall would be built, up to 5 ft (1.5 m) or so in height; the shape, size and direction being maintained by two frames with straining cords between. The wall would be built sloping inwards towards the top for extra stability, and two stones wide with occasional through or tie stones inserted through the full width to bind them together. Smaller stones would be used to fill any gaps in the centre or at the sides. Finally, large flat stones were used at the top to level the wall before a coping or capping was added made up of flat, rounded stones placed on edge.

The Forestry Commission

The Forestry Commission was set up in 1919 by the Government of the day with the objective of reducing the United Kingdom's dependence on overseas supplies of timber; this was to be achieved by the building-up of forests, some owned by the State and some under private ownership. This still remains the overall policy of the Commission. Whilst many walkers are critical of the afforestation that has taken place in North Wales and elsewhere, it should be remembered that even today this country has less land producing tree crops than almost any other country in Europe and imports more timber and timber products than any country in the world.

Generally in North Wales the upper limit of economic afforestation is around 1800 ft (550 m) and the forests therefore have been planted in the valleys, on low hills or on the lower slopes of mountains. The trees are raised in nurseries owned by the Commission, usually being transplanted into their final quarters as two to three year old seedlings up to 24 in (60 cm) in height at a planting distance currently of 6½ ft (2 m); most of the existing forest was planted at spacing between 4½–6 ft (1.3–1.8 m). Planting is carried out at an amazingly fast rate, usually between 500 and 1500 trees per day for each man. Comparatively little cultivation is needed over the years. It is the usual practice wherever possible to plough before planting with furrows set about 6½ ft (2 m) apart and to weed afterwards; thinning starts at twenty to twenty-five years after planting, the thinnings providing a valuable source of income, and continues to final felling at around fifty to sixty years. About 12% of the Park is afforested at the present time.

The vast majority of Commission and private plantings have been of conifers, which provide softwoods. This reflects current demand in Britain, is more profitable and in any case is the only one possible on much of the high northern land available for afforestation. Broad-leaved trees such as oak and beech require good soil conditions to grow economically. However, natural growth of oak, birch, alder and willow can be widespread particularly along stream sides and rocky outcrops. This is encouraged for landscaping reasons, at the same time increasing the diversity of wildlife habitats. Additional planting of broad-leaves is sometimes necessary where natural growth is unlikely to come in. The only native timber-producing conifer is the Scots Pine which is planted widely, but this has the disadvantage of slow growth. As a result, coniferous trees from other countries have been introduced into the forests, in particular the Sitka Spruce and the Lodgepole Pine, both from western North America.

In addition to its work as a producer of timber, the Commission is very active in research to promote good forestry, in providing an information service to the owners of private woodlands and in the administration of schemes to help private forestry.

The Commission has also been active in providing recreational facilities within its forests, such as car-parks, campsites, nature trails, exhibitions, arboreta, forest gardens, etc. In particular eight areas have been designated as Forest Parks, of which one, the Snowdonia Forest Park, is in North Wales. These are areas of forest and open moor, open to the public for recreation. Generally, within the forest areas of a Park the public is free to walk any path or forest road.

The Snowdonia Forest Park was established in 1937 and consists of Gwydyr Forest, around Betws-y-Coed, and Beddgelert Forest to the north-west of Beddgelert, a total area of almost 20,000 acres (9710 hectares).

Hafod and Hendref

The word 'hafod' (or 'hafotty') is common among the place-names of North Wales, a reminder of the old method of farming when the farmer moved his cattle to the higher pastures during the summer, living nearby with his family in a small 'summer dwelling' or 'hafod'. The main farm in the valley was the 'hendref' or 'winter dwelling', the fields there being used during the cattle's absence to produce hay for winter feed. The last record of this method of farming (called transhumance) in England and Wales was in Snowdonia in 1862. The hafodydd themselves have fallen gradually into ruin or, in some cases in lower and more accessible areas, been converted into permanent farms.

THE ICE AGE IN NORTH WALES

The Ice Age (known to geologists as the Pleistocene Period) began two million years ago and ended about 10,000 years ago. During that time there were four major periods of intense cold, separated by spells of warmer weather, probably similar to that which we have today. During the cold periods great sheets of ice, thousands of feet thick, advanced southwards from Scandinavia down the Scottish and Irish seas to reach North Wales, whilst in the higher mountains of the region permanent snow formed and accumulated and bred glaciers which flowed down the mountainsides, usually taking the easy lines offered by the valleys of mountain streams. As the ice flowed, the mass slowly rotated grinding away the bedrock into a huge hollow, whilst that frozen to the backwall plucked away the rock to form a steep rear wall.

Eventually, as snow accumulated, the glacier reached the main river valley and flowing along it straightened its course, by shearing away side ridges, and smoothed and deepened its floor, until finally at a point when further flow could no longer be sustained, the glacier ended. There a huge spoil heap of debris was formed, plucked and scraped from the valley walls and carried down by the ice flow; this heap is now called a terminal moraine.

As the ice retreated back up the valley at the end of the Ice Age it left behind the terminal moraine and strewed further rock debris throughout the valley floor. Occasionally the ice paused and formed further moraines before its retreat recommenced. Tributary glaciers would be left behind, high up on the walls of the main valley.

10,000 years is very short in geological terms and relatively little change has taken place in North Wales due to weathering since the end of the Ice Age. The general impression therefore is of a region recently vacated by the glaciers. Cymoedd with their steep rear wall and characteristic 'scooped' shape cut deeply into most mountain masses (usually lakes have formed into the cwm hollows), the main valleys are straight with truncated side ridges and of characteristic U-shape, whilst moraines, 'perched' boulders and ice-smoothed bedrock can be found everywhere.

THE NATURE CONSERVANCY COUNCIL

The Council, set up by Government legislation in 1973, is responsible for nature conservation in Great Britain. In particular, it has responsibility for the management of National Nature

Reserves. These are either owned or leased by the Council, or in some cases are the result of an agreement between the Council and the owners whereby the ownership remains unchanged but is subject to certain conditions relating to land use. Certain Reserves are open to the public, while access to the remainder is allowed only by permit, available from the appropriate local regional office.

The Council is also responsible for notifying Sites of Special Scientific Interest (SSSIs). In SSSI areas, owners/occupiers are obliged to consult the Council before carrying out operations which may be damaging to the scientific interest of the site. The provisions of the 1981 Wildlife and Countryside Act have now made habitat conservation a matter of criminal law. Under the same Act, the Council is the licensing authority in relation to species of birds, animals and plants which have been given special protection and also has specific responsibilities in relation to bats. Finally, the Council acts as an advisor to the Government, local authorities and individuals, and initiates research on conservation matters.

There are sixteen National Nature Reserves and forty-two SSSIs in the Snowdonia National Park. Of the Reserves in the Park permits are *not* required to enter:

Cader Idris (open mountain only)
Coedydd Aber
Cwm Idwal
Yr Wyddfa-Snowdon
Coed Ganllwyd
Coedydd Maentwrog
Rhinog

Rock Climbing

Early rock climbing in this country was carried out by mountaineers who regarded it merely as practice for the more serious climbing of the Alps. British rock climbing as a pursuit in itself is normally considered to have begun with the ascent of the Napes Needle, a rock spire on Great Gable in the Lake District, by W. P. Haskett Smith in 1886, but others were also taking the first tentative steps around that time. The early years of rock climbing towards the end of the last century are usually referred to as the 'gully era' because the main attack was on *gullies*, the wide deep clefts which split the crags. Gradually, however, attention shifted to the open faces themselves — at first to *slabs* (rock at a low-angle) and then to *walls* (vertical or near vertical rock) and to more *exposed* climbs (i.e., with a considerable drop). In North Wales standards increased considerably in the years both before World War II, due particularly to Colin Kirkus and John Menlove Edwards, and afterwards in the 1950s by Joe Brown, Don Whillans and others. Nowadays, there are more people climbing than ever before and also more who can climb to a very high standard. As a result new routes are constantly being discovered and standards continue to increase. Clogwyn du'r Arddu, the Black Cliff, on Snowdon (known to climbers as 'Cloggy') has been the setting for a number of major climbs by the great climbers.

Climbers on the Idwal Slabs (Route 8)

Usually in this country on major crags, a climbing party will consist of two or three climbers of whom only one will climb at a time. The *leader* will ascend the rock until a *stance* is reached where he will *belay*, i.e., attach himself with a sling to a natural rock spike or to an artificial aid such as a *nut* (wedge-shaped metal) jammed into a crack; the *second man* will then climb up to the stance protected from a fall by the rope to the leader. The leader will then continue to a higher stance where he will belay, the third man then joining his companion. This process is repeated to the top of the cliff. The sections of rock between stances are called *pitches*. Generally, therefore, the rope is used for protection in ascent and not for actual climbing and a fall should be limited to only one climber.

Climbs are graded for difficulty. The grades are easy, moderate, difficult, very difficult, severe, very severe, extremely severe; each of the grades is then subdivided into 'mild' or 'hard'. A numerical grading is also used. Rock climbers have developed a vocabulary of their own and much specialized equipment is produced to meet their needs. Guides have been written describing routes on the major crags and many of the cottages in Snowdonia have been bought for use as climbing club huts.

Search and Rescue Helicopters in Snowdonia

No. 22 (Search and Rescue) Squadron of the Royal Air Force maintains five detached flights of aircraft around the coast of Britain, all of which fly Wessex helicopters. 'C' Flight of 22 Squadron arrived at RAF Valley, near Holyhead on Anglesey, in 1955. It is primarily concerned with the rescue of aircrew who have ejected from their aircraft, but it works in close liaison with HM Coastguard, the RNLI, Police and Mountain Rescue Teams and as a result is often called out to help civilians, whether walkers or climbers in the mountains or swimmers and yachtsmen along the coast.

Two yellow Wessex helicopters are available for this purpose on call twenty-four hours every day. In daylight one helicopter and crew are maintained at fifteen minutes readiness, the second taking over when the first is called out; at night the readiness time rises to one hour as more detailed flight planning is necessary before take-off. (In fact, during the day the helicopters are usually airborne within four minutes of a call being received.) The Wessex helicopter is a Westland twin-turbine version of the American Sikorsky S58. Since 1955 over 4000 rescue missions have been flown.

The Sheep Dog

Statistics for 1973 give a sheep population of nearly 900,000 for the Snowdonia National Park. The management of this enormous number of animals would be quite impossible without the help of one inhabitant of North Wales, the sheep dog.

Although dogs have been used to control sheep since Roman times, great numbers of men were needed to gather sheep from the hillsides during the eighteenth century. The Border Collie, probably introduced into Wales from Westmorland during the early nineteenth century, transformed the work of the shepherd. Chosen for their ability to handle sheep and not for their looks, Border Collies vary both in size and appearance; but most dogs are long-haired, black with white collar and chest band, square-set ears and long sloping tail. Neither pedigree nor appearance are reliable guides to the value of a dog, in the last analysis it is only their performance that counts.

Training begins at about six months and will normally be completed in about another six, but no two dogs are alike and methods have to be modified accordingly. Commands are given by shouts or whistles, most Welsh farmers preferring the latter, with a different set for each dog. The basic commands for general work are: **1** Stop, **2** Go anticlockwise around the sheep, **3** Go clockwise around the sheep, **4** Come onto your sheep, **5** Come to me; to which may be added further commands for more specialized movements.

The sheep dog is at its busiest from spring to autumn, when the main tasks of gathering and shedding (collecting together and sorting) are carried out, but there is always some work throughout the year. In severe winters of heavy snowfall sheep become buried in deep drifts and the Border Collie is then invaluable for finding them. The severe losses of 1946–47, 1962–63, and 1978–79 would have been even greater without their help.

Sheep Farming

The raising of sheep is the only form of farming possible on the large areas of thin and poor soil which make up most of the North Wales uplands, and is therefore the main activity of hill farms throughout Snowdonia.

A typical hill farm will be made up of three areas: the open mountainside, often rocky and of poor pasture, which can be used only for summer grazing; the 'ffridd', a smaller but still substantial area nearer to the farm and separated from the higher ground by a long mountain wall, where the pasture is better and which can be used for the overwintering of older ewes; and finally the low fields around the farm kept under cultivation where hay or occasionally other crops can be grown.

Lambing starts in late March and continues until well into April in the fields around the farmhouse, each ewe usually producing a single lamb. After lambing, the ewe and her lamb are driven up the hillside, first to the 'ffridd' and then in May onto the open mountainside. The concentration of the flock upon the mountain is low, one ewe and her lamb to each acre being typical, each ewe keeping to her own small area of mountainside.

During June–July the flock is driven down from the mountain to the low fields where the older sheep are sheared, each ewe providing about 2–3 lb (0.9–1.4 kg) of wool. After shearing the ewes are dipped against scab and ticks, before being driven back with their lambs to the mountain.

At the end of the summer in September the sheep are again collected into the lowland fields. Female lambs, now well grown, are separated from the flock and sent down to lowland farms, such as in Anglesey, where the winters are milder, for overwintering; they are brought back again to the highland farms at the end of March. Male lambs are sold off either for immediate slaughter or for slaughter after further fattening; although a few will be kept for breeding purposes.

During the winter the breeding flock of older ewes stays near to the farm on the lowland fields or on the 'ffridd'. From around the third week of October they run with the rams, normally about one ram for every fifty to sixty ewes, and the breeding cycle begins again.

Each ewe is held on an upland farm for four summers, then it is sold, usually to lowland farms where it will live and produce lambs for one to two years more.

The Welsh Mountain Sheep is the dominant breed within the Park, able to live on the sparse grass of the hills and to withstand the heavy rain of the region. It is relatively small in

NOTE:
Every year considerable losses are caused to farmers in Snowdonia, and elsewhere, by dogs which chase sheep and lambs. For that reason domestic dogs are not welcome in Snowdonia unless they are kept under close control or, even better, on a lead.
Lambs, however weak or forlorn they may look, should not be handled as this may lead to the mother sheep deserting them.

body with soft, fine wool, and can be recognized by its white face and legs and by its characteristic narrow-shouldered, long-necked appearance. The rams, but not the ewes, have strong curved horns.

Signposts and Stiles

Highway Authorities have a duty under the Countryside Act of 1968 to erect signs at any point where a path with public right of way leaves a metalled road. The County Surveyor's Department of Gwynedd County Council is the Highway Authority for the Snowdonia National Park. As a result a large number of signs have been erected in recent years. The most common are long metal rectangular arrows, green with white edging, bearing the words 'Llwybr Cyhoeddus' on one side and 'Public Footpath' on the other. These are being phased out at the present time and replaced by shorter metal rectangular arrows, green with a white 'walking man' on each side.

The Snowdonia National Park Authority has also erected a number of marker posts indicating routes through enclosed land; these posts are normally made from wood with the figure of a pedestrian and a direction arrow routed out of the wood, the symbols being painted white. A variety of 'unofficial' waymarks are also used in hill country; these include wooden posts, upright slabs of rock, cairns, white painted arrows, etc. On some very popular routes special markers have been erected, e.g., rock monoliths on Snowdon.

A considerable number of wooden ladder stiles (several hundred), usually with metal gauze on the steps, have been placed at strategic spots over walls and fences around the Park, the majority by the Authority with the agreement of local farmers. The work of erecting these stiles is still continuing.

Short lengths of fence have been placed in appropriate positions alongside some popular paths to prevent walkers taking short cuts. This is done where any widening or proliferation of paths would cause damage to the environment.

Slate

Derelict slate quarries and mines are a characteristic feature of North Wales. The towns of Bethesda, Llanberis and Blaenau Ffestiniog are dominated by them, but smaller mines and trial levels are to be found throughout the region, even well up into the hills. The slate industry forms an integral part of the history and the heritage of the region.

The slate beds were laid down originally as muds during the Cambrian, Ordovician and Silurian periods, between 400 and 600 million years ago, when North Wales was submerged for long periods of time beneath the sea. In the stagnant conditions of the sea floor this fine mud gradually accumulated to form beds and then became overlaid with other deposits, either sedimentary or of igneous origin such as lava or volcanic ash. Under the immense pressure generated by these higher deposits the early sediments compacted into a soft rock, which is now called sedimentary on account of its origin. In some cases, however, where the sediment and extremes of temperature and pressure were suitable, a more profound change took place in the physical form of the rock and a hard slate was formed (blue, grey, or purple in colour depending upon the nature of the original deposit). The small plate-like particles of the deposit packed together and orientated at 90° to the direction of pressure; this orientation producing a cleavage in the slate so that when struck sharply on its edge a block will split cleanly into thin smooth sheets. This ability to form sheets, its attractive appearance and its high resistance to weathering have made slate a commodity useful to man.

Some of the finest slate in the world was formed in this way under the Welsh hills. Some of it was eroded away long ago, whilst in some areas it lies inaccessibly deep beneath the ground, but at a few places where it approached the surface, extraction was possible and vigorously pursued, producing the huge quarries and mines which are now so much a feature of North Wales.

The great Cambrian slate-belt runs for about 16 miles (26 km) to the south-west from Bethesda to Penygroes and contains several huge quarries, notably the Penrhyn Quarry at Bethesda, the Dinorwic Quarry at Llanberis and the Dorothea in the Nantlle Valley. At both the Penrhyn and the Dinorwic the beds emerged steeply onto the mountain sides and extraction was carried out by cutting terraces (galleries) each about 60–75 ft (18–23 m) high into the hillside, whilst in the Nantlle Valley deep pits were dug to extract the slate. A second important belt of slate crosses the area of Blaenau Ffestiniog; here the beds lie at about 30° from the horizontal and the slate has had to be extracted by mining techniques. A third region is around Corris and Abergynolwyn and a fourth is to the east at Corwen and Llangollen.

A few of the old quarries and mines are still put to use. Some slate is produced at Llechwedd; the Dinorwic now houses the machine hall of the largest pumped-storage power station in Europe and the quarry workshops there are used as the Welsh Slate Museum which is part of the National Museum of Wales, whilst at Blaenau Ffestiniog there are two mining museums. But now, most of the old workings are deserted, left only to the wind, the sheep and to the occasional farmer or rambler.

The Welsh Black

Although the predominant farm animal of the Park is undoubtedly the sheep, many farmers also keep a herd of cattle. The most important breed is the Welsh Black. This is one of the most ancient, but the modern animal is a result of interbreeding between a number of local types, in particular those of North and South Wales. It is a dual-purpose animal, kept for its milk and for its beef, and valued for its hardiness and for its ability to produce good yields of milk, under the relatively harsh conditions of North Wales. The animals are horned with short black hair and are generally docile.

The Welsh Language

The 1971 Census gave the population of the Park as 25,054 of which 17,724 were Welsh-speaking, i.e., 71% although the proportion varied considerably from one area to another. South Meirionnydd with 59% had the lowest proportion whilst east Meirionnydd had the highest with 88%. As a comparison, only 21% of the entire population of Wales spoke Welsh; of the counties, Gwynedd had the highest with 62% (most of the population of Gwynedd live outside the Park), Dyfed was next with 50% and the remaining counties had only between 11 and 21%. The number speaking Welsh has been falling steadily throughout the past century.

Wild Goats

Over 200 years ago, according to contemporary accounts, goats were kept in substantial numbers in Snowdonia, but this practice declined in the latter half of the eighteenth century. The goats that can be seen nowadays above the Ogwen Valley and in the Rhinogydd and elsewhere are their descendants. They are described as 'ferral goats', i.e., wild animals descended from originally domesticated stock.

Selected Walks in the Snowdonia National Park

Introduction to the Route Descriptions

1. ACCESS (see page 186)

The routes described later have, as far as is known, been walked for a long time without objection and it is not expected therefore that any difficulties will be encountered. Nevertheless, they do in some cases cross country over which there is, strictly speaking, no legal right of way, and in such cases the responsibility must lie with the walker to obtain any necessary

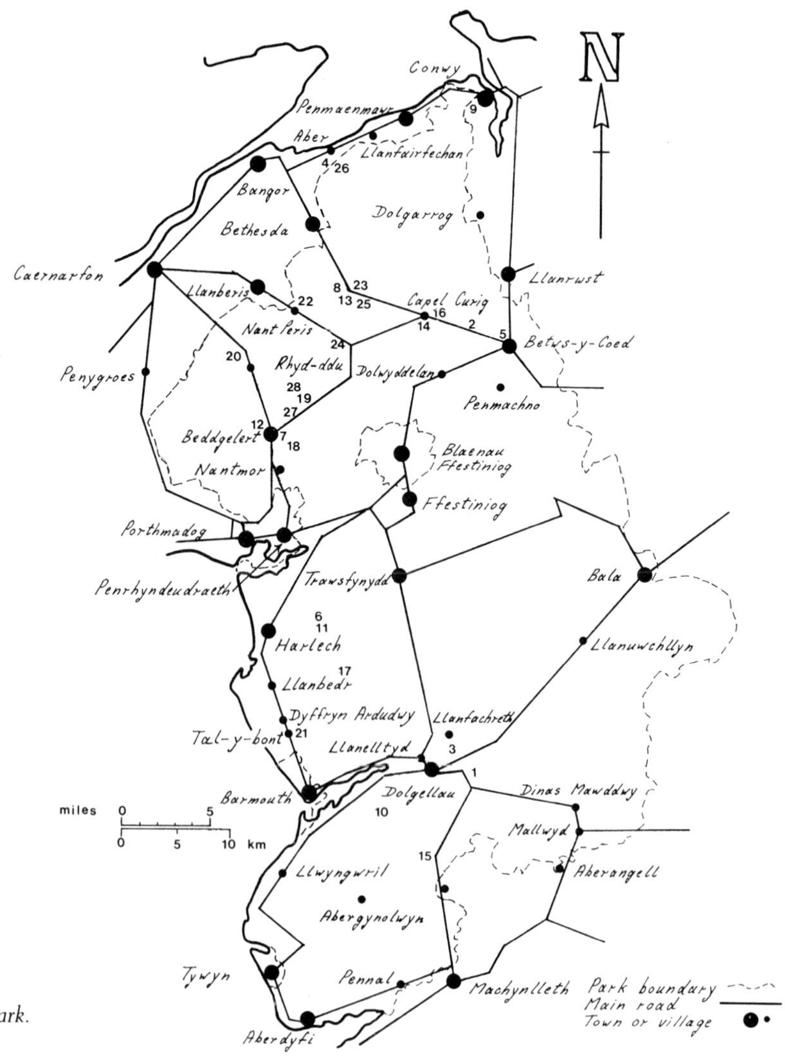

FIGURE 1 The Snowdonia National Park. The numbers indicate the approximate starting points for the routes described.

permission before crossing such land. In particular, 'short cuts' should not be taken that could cause annoyance to local people.

2. ASCENT — The amount of climbing involved in each route has been estimated from Outdoor Leisure or 1:50 000 maps as appropriate and should be regarded as approximate only.

3. CAR-PARKS — The nearest public car-park is given. There will be many places where a car can be parked by the wayside, but it must be done with care, as indiscriminate parking can be a great nuisance to local people.

4. INTERESTING FEATURES ON THE ROUTE — The best position for seeing these is indicated both in the route descriptions and on the maps by *(1)*, *(2)*, etc.

5. LENGTH — These are strictly 'map miles' estimated from the Outdoor Leisure maps; no attempt has been made to take into account any ascent or descent involved.

6. MAPS — The maps are drawn to a scale of approximately 1:25 000 (see

FIGURE 2 *Signs used on detailed route maps*

page 25) and all names are as given on the Outdoor Leisure maps. Field boundaries in particular should be taken as a 'best description'. The maps have been drawn in the main, so that the route goes from the bottom to the top of a page. This will enable the reader to 'line up' the map whilst still holding the book in the normal reading position. The arrow on each map points to grid north. The scale of some small features has been slightly exaggerated for clarity. For easy cross-reference the relevant Outdoor Leisure and Landranger sheets are indicated on each map.

7. ROUTE DESCRIPTION

The letters 'L' and 'R' stand for left and right respectively. Where these are used for changes of direction then they imply a turn of about 90° when facing in the direction of the walk. 'Half L' and 'half R' indicate a half-turn, i.e. approximately 45°, and 'back half L' or 'back half R' indicate three quarter-turns, i.e. about 135°. PFS stands for 'Public Footpath Sign', PBS for 'Public Bridleway Sign' and OS for 'Ordnance Survey'.

To avoid constant repetition, it should be assumed that all stiles and gates mentioned in the route description are to be crossed (unless there is a specific statement otherwise).

8. STANDARD OF THE ROUTES

The briefest examination of the route descriptions that follow will show that the routes described cover an enormous range of both length and of difficulty; some of the easy routes at least can be undertaken by a family party, with care, at almost any time of the year while the hardest routes are only really suitable for experienced fell-walkers who are both fit and well-equipped. Any walker therefore who is contemplating following a route should make sure before starting that it is within their ability.

It is difficult in practice, however, to assess the difficulty of any route because it is dependent upon a number of factors and will in any case vary considerably from day to day with the weather. Any consideration of weather conditions must, of course, be left to the walker himself (but read the section on safety first). Apart from that, it is probably best to attempt an overall assessment of difficulty based upon the length, amount of ascent and descent, problems of route-finding and finally, upon the roughness of the terrain.

Each of the routes has therefore been given a grading based upon a consideration of these factors. A general description of each grade follows.

Easy (1): generally short walks (up to 5 miles, 8 km) over well-defined paths, with no problems of route-finding. Some climbing may be involved, but progress is mostly over fairly gradual slopes with only short sections of more difficult ground. The paths may, however, sometimes run alongside cliffs, streams or steep slopes where care should be taken.

Moderate (2): rather longer walks (up to about 10 miles, 16 km), mostly over paths, but with sections where route-finding will be more difficult. Mountain summits may be reached with climbing over steeper and rougher ground.

More strenuous (3): perhaps longer walks (10–20 miles, 16–32 km) with prolonged spells of climbing. Some rough ground calling for good route-finding ability, perhaps with stretches of scrambling with some exposure.

Very strenuous (4): only for the few, involving long distances (over 20 miles, 32 km), with a considerable amount of climbing over difficult ground.

The walks are arranged in order of increasing difficulty so that Route 1 is the easiest and Route 28 is the hardest.

Finally, a summary of each walk is given at the head of each section with information on the distance, amount of climbing and any special difficulties, such as scrambling, that will be met along the way.

9. STARTING AND FINISHING POINTS

The majority of the routes are circular in order to avoid any problems with transport when the walk is completed.

The location of each starting and finishing point is given by the number of the appropriate Landranger (1:50 000) map with a six figure grid reference; thus (124–761180) indicates grid reference 761180 which can be found on Landranger sheet no. 124. The starting points are also shown on figure 1.

10. TIME FOR COMPLETION

The usual method of estimating the length of time needed for a walk is by Naismith's Rule: 'For ordinary walking allow one hour for every 3 miles (5 km) and add one hour for every 2000 feet (600 m) of ascent; for backpacking with a heavy load allow one hour for every 2½ miles (4 km) and one hour for every 1500 feet (450 m) of ascent'. However, for many this tends to be over-optimistic and it is better for each walker to form an assessment of his own performance over one or two walks. Naismith's Rule also makes no allowance for rest or food stops or for the influence of weather conditions.

1·1

The Torrent Walk

STARTING AND FINISHING POINT
Take the Machynlleth road from Dolgellau (A470) turning L along the B4416 to Brithdir after 2 miles (3 km). The walk starts on L about 200 yd (180 m) after the bridge (124-761180).
LENGTH
1½ miles (2.4 km)
ASCENT
375 ft (110 m)

Opposite *Afon Clywedog*

The last mile of the Afon Clywedog, to its junction with the Afon Wnion, is by a beautiful wooded gorge, through which the river flows in a superb series of waterfalls and watershoots. This short and easy walk along a clear path beside the river gives wonderful views throughout.

Route Description (Map 1)

From the small gate on the Brithdir road (sign 'Llwybr-y-Torrent, Torrent Walk') follow a path down to the river and over a bridge. Continue ahead downstream with the river to your R. The way is absolutely clear along the L bank of the river through lovely deciduous woods to a small gate on the minor road at Clywedog. Return by the same route.

Steps have been constructed on the steepest sections and short lengths of fence placed for safety where the drop to the river becomes more considerable; but, with reasonable care, particularly of children, nowhere is it anything but easy and safe.

MAP 1

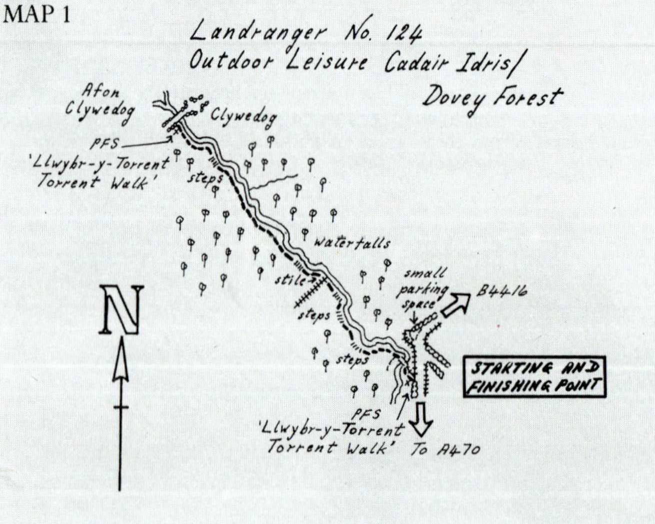

1·2

Through the Llugwy Gorge

STARTING POINT
Ty-hyll (the Ugly House) (115-756575)
FINISHING POINT
Pont-y-Pair bridge, Betws-y-Coed (115-792567)
LENGTH
$2\frac{3}{4}$ miles (4.5 km)
ASCENT
100 ft (30 m)

An extremely attractive walk along the Llugwy Gorge past the Ugly House, the Swallow Falls and the Miners' Bridge, including a stretch of the Gwydyr Forest. The Swallow Falls are probably the most popular tourist attraction in Wales, but almost everybody else will be on the opposite bank, where a charge is made for admission.

Route Description (Map 2)

From the Ugly House *(1)*, cross the minor road and pass the small private car-park to the end of the bridge (PFS). Go down the steps on to the river bank and walk downstream with the river to the R, soon crossing a stile into a wood. The path continues in the same direction, gradually rising above the river until the Swallow Falls *(2)* can be seen below. A superb path runs across the steep wooded hillside above the falls with rocks above and a steep fall down to the R towards the river. Despite this spectacular setting, however, there is no real danger as a guarding fence has been erected throughout.

Where the fence ends, reach open ground. The wide path to the L goes to the tea-gardens at Allt-isaf which can be used for a pleasant break. Otherwise, continue in the same direction along a narrow path crossing a small stream and through a plantation of young trees. After the plantation take the wide path which rises through mature trees to a forest track at the top *(3)*. Here turn R to a road where turn R again. After about 50 yards (45 m) drop down to the R on to a lower and extremely pleasant path through the forest. The path is level to start with, but later descends steeply towards the river; carry on, crossing two small bridges near the river, until a splendid fenced viewpoint is reached overlooking rapids. Rise L up to the road.

Go R along the road for about 60 yards (55 m), then leave the road to the R dropping down by a fence to the Miners' Bridge *(4)*. Do not cross, but continue downstream on the same side of

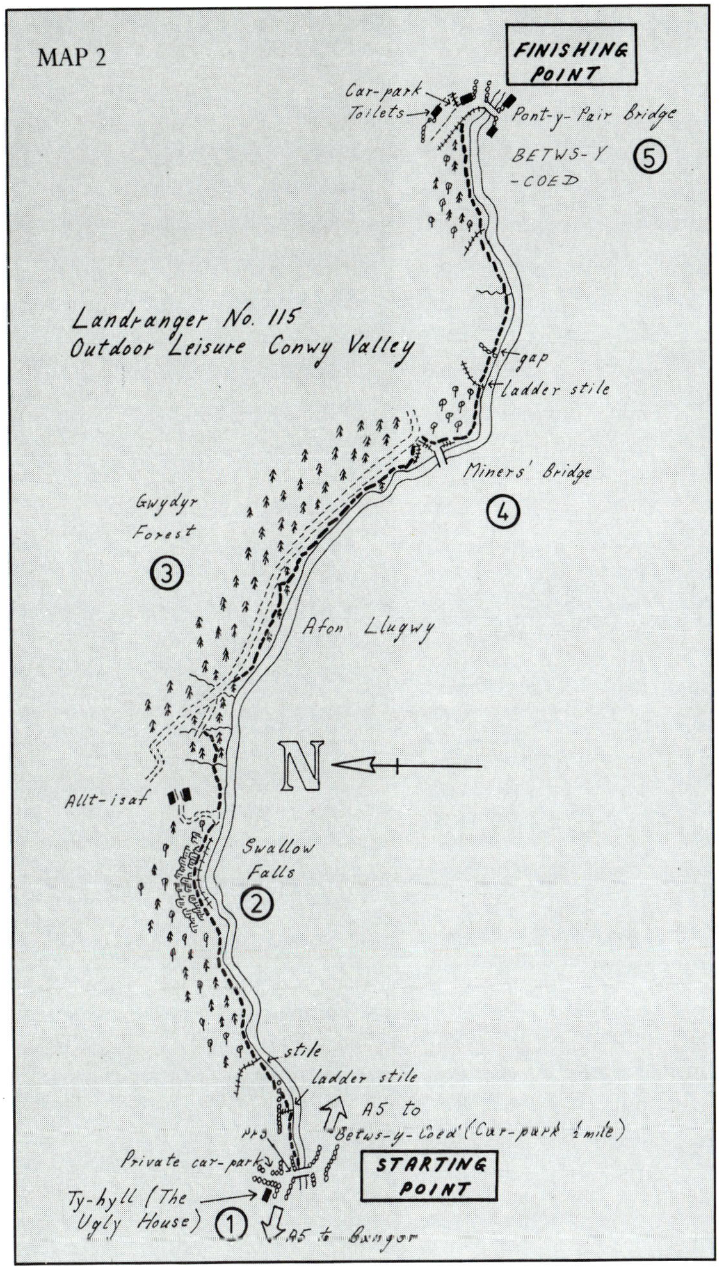

the river, soon leaving the wood over a ladder stile. Continue along the bank, later crossing a fence, until a road is reached opposite the car-park at the Pont-y-Pair bridge *(5)* at Betws-y-Coed.

1 Ty-hyll, the Ugly House

The Ugly House, which stands on the Capel Curig side of the bridge over the Llugwy, lives up to its name. A rough and primitive building of enormous strength, with slate roof and walls of unusual thickness, it was built about 1475. No mortar was used.

2 *The Swallow Falls*

A survey in 1975 showed that the Swallow Falls were visited by about 690,000 people annually. The majority of visitors approach the Falls from the road on the south side, where a car-park has been provided, paying a fee for the privilege. The Falls can also be viewed from the north bank, free of charge, using the public right-of-way; here the view is admittedly poorer but the walking much more exciting.

George Borrow, who visited North Wales in 1854 and wrote of his experiences in *Wild Wales*, which is now a classic still sold in local shops, described the Falls as follows: 'The Fall of the Swallow is not a majestic single fall, but a succession of small ones. First there are a number of little foaming torrents, bursting through rocks about twenty yards above the promontory, on which I stood. Then came two beautiful rolls of white water, dashing into a pool a little way above the promontory; then there is a swirl of water round its corner into a pool below on its right, black as death and seemingly of great depth; then a rush through a very narrow outlet into another pool, from which the water clamours away down the glen. Such is the Rhaiadr y Wennol, or Swallow Fall; called so from the rapidity with which the waters rush and skip along'.

3 *The Gwydyr Forest*

The walk passes through a lovely section of the forest, the property of the Forestry Commission. See pages 13 and 94.

4 *The Miners' Bridge*

The Miners' Bridge over the Llugwy is inclined as a ladder from one bank to the other at an angle of about 30° to the horizontal. The bridge originally served as a convenient route for miners living nearby at Pentre-du, south of the river, to reach their work in the lead mines situated on the higher ground to the north. The present bridge was erected about 1983 and is the fifth or sixth on the site.

5 *Pont-y-Pair Bridge, Betws-y-Coed*

'The Bridge of the Cauldron', spanning the turbulent Llugwy by a series of five arches at the western end of Betws-y-Coed, is of uncertain date. It may be fifteenth century, built by a local man named Howel, but it may also be the work of Inigo Jones about 200 years later in the seventeenth. There are fine rapids upstream from the bridge — hence its name.

Afon Llugwy

1·3

THE PRECIPICE WALK

STARTING AND FINISHING POINT
Car-park at Saith groesffordd (124-746212). Leave Dolgellau on the A494 to Bala, branching L $\frac{1}{4}$ mile (400 m) after the bridge. Follow minor road for $2\frac{1}{2}$ miles (4 km) through three junctions to reach car-park.
LENGTH
$3\frac{1}{2}$ miles (5.5 km)
ASCENT
125 ft (40 m)

A short and easy walk with little climbing around the two summits of Foel Cynwch and Foel Faner and the lovely Llyn Cynwch. For much of the route, the way is a narrow path running across the steep hillside high above the Afon Mawddach with superb views over the valley and the great forest of Coed y Brenin beyond.

This path is not a public right of way, but access has been granted by the Nannau Estate since 1890. The National Park Authority has provided stiles, waste bins and information boards around the walk. This should not be confused with the New Precipice Walk which is further to the west near Borthwnog.

ROUTE DESCRIPTION (Map 3)

Leave the car-park and turn L along the road past an Information Board. After a short distance turn L through a gate (sign 'Precipice Walk') and walk along a path between conifers.

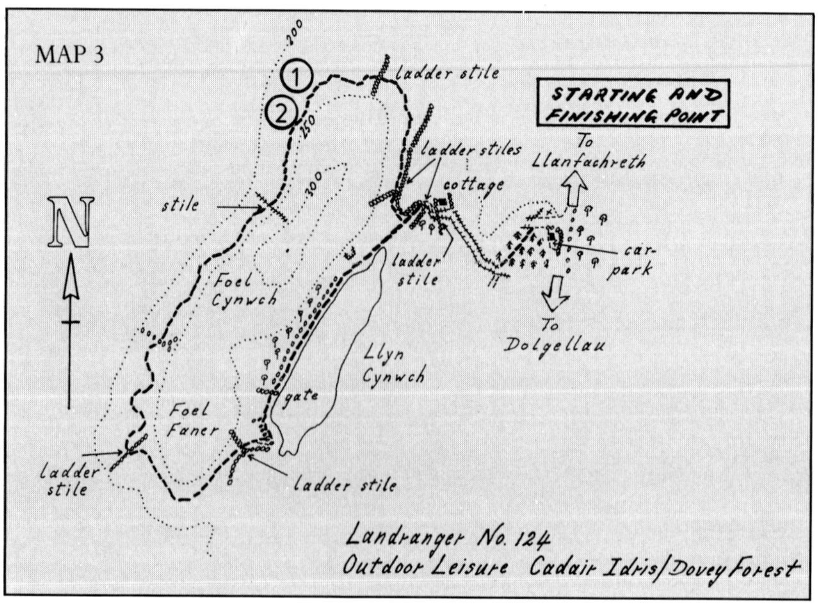

The path soon bends R and continues between fences to a cottage. Turn L before the cottage, up to a ladder stile. The path turns R after the stile and then bends to the L to reach a second ladder stile. Cross and shortly afterwards take the R fork at a path junction. The path climbs to a wall and bends R with it; continue with this wall keeping it to your R, crossing a further ladder stile.

The path from there is clear and follows the 800 ft (245 m) contour around Foel Cynwch and then further along around Foel Faner. Magnificent views open up as you progress along this walk, over the Mawddach Valley *(1)* and beyond to the Coed y Brenin Forest *(2)*. For a short distance the slope below the path is particularly steep, hence Precipice Walk.

Eventually the path bends away from the main valley crossing a ladder stile, and runs along the hillside to the L of a small dry valley. Cross another ladder stile and continue to the lake Llyn Cynwch, there cross a low wall and turn L. Walk along the L side of the lake to rejoin the original path at a junction. Return to the car-park.

1 The Gold Mines of the Mawddach

The gold belt of North Wales extended in an arc, about one mile wide along the valley of the Afon Mawddach from its estuary at Barmouth to its upper reaches within the Coed y Brenin Forest. Although some gold may have been extracted in this region prior to the nineteenth century, the industry really began in 1844 with the discovery of gold at the Cwm-heisian Mines, which were being worked at that time for lead, and ended to all intents and purposes during World War I. A total of nearly 130,000 oz of gold was extracted during that period, of which the vast bulk came from two mines: the Clogau, between Barmouth and Dolgellau near the village of Bontddu, and Gwynfynydd, at the northern extremity of the field. Both mines were in continuous production from around 1890 to their closures in 1911 and 1916 respectively.

The gold occurs as very fine yellow particles embedded in veins of quartz, called lodes. The distribution of gold is by no means uniform, which accounts for the violent fluctuations in the output from the mines (and hence their profitability). A tunnel or level was driven along the lode until a gold-rich area was discovered, this would then be dug out, the extracted ore being taken up to the surface in small waggons. The ore was crushed to free the metallic particles, which were then separated from the waste by amalgamation with mercury. The amount of waste was enormous; in the case of the Clogau, for instance, between 1900 and 1910 inclusive, its most successful years, no less than 108,329 tons of quartz had to be crushed to produce 54,970 oz of gold, a ratio of 52,972:1.

The wedding rings of Queen Elizabeth the Queen Mother (1923), The Queen (1947), The Princess Margaret (1960), The Princess Anne (1973) and The Princess of Wales (1981) were made from the same nugget of Welsh gold, which came from the Clogau. In 1981 the Royal British Legion presented the Queen with a sample of Welsh gold weighing 36g and it was from this that the wedding ring of the Duchess of York was made in 1986.

2 *Coed y Brenin Forest (The Forest of the King)*

Coed y Brenin Forest, owned by the Forestry Commission, covers an area of over 23,200 acres (9400 ha) round the valleys of the Afon Mawddach and its tributaries. Most of the land for the forest was purchased from the Vaughan family, owners of the local estate of Nannau — hence its original name of Vaughan Forest — and planting commenced in 1922. The name was changed to its present form in 1935 to commemorate the Silver Jubilee of George V. There are over 100 miles (160 km) of forest roads and paths open to walkers, of which approximately half have been waymarked, a nature trail, a mountain bothy, a small arboretum at Glasdir and a Visitor Centre near Maesgwm, 8 miles (13 km) north of Dolgellau on the A470.

View towards The Precipice Walk

1·4

To the Rhaeadr-fawr, The Aber Falls

STARTING AND FINISHING POINT
Bontnewydd (115-662720). From A55, turn up minor road in Aber by Aber Falls Hotel and Garage, and immediately R (sign on road). Continue up road for about ¾ mile (1.2 km) to small car-park by bridge over river; there is a further and larger car-park across the bridge.
LENGTH
3 miles (5 km)
ASCENT
500 ft (150 m)

A short but exceedingly pleasant walk which follows the river to the Rhaeadr-fawr, a spectacular waterfall 120 ft (37 m) high. Return by the same route or by a delightful path through a coniferous forest.

Route Description (Map 4)

From the small car-park by the bridge over the Afon Aber go through the small gate to the L of the Park Information Board *(1)* (footpath sign to Aber Falls). Keep on the R side of the stream to a footbridge, cross and go through the gate on the far side into the farm road beyond. Turn R along the farm road and continue ahead, ignoring the farm road bending back to the L. Further along, bend round to the R of a small cottage. Soon after the cottage, where the farm road goes L and becomes faint, go ahead on a path through a gap in a wall and later through a gate. The falls are now directly ahead.

You can return, of course, by the same route but a much better way is to use a lovely woodland path which crosses the hillside to the R and which will give about the same distance. For this alternative path return to the gate, go through, then turn R over a ladder stile and climb away from the falls up the slope half L along the obvious path (the path is marked by short posts with blue painted tops). Eventually at the end of the rise go over a stile into a wood and follow the path ahead, keeping L at a path junction (do not follow the blue markers here, which are for the R-hand path). This delightful path through the forest is quite clear throughout. Eventually leave the wood over a stile and on through a wall gap to the R of a sheepfold. Continue in the same direction with a fence to your R to reach the farm road that you walked along earlier on your way to the falls. Turn R along it back to the car-park.

The Aber Falls in winter

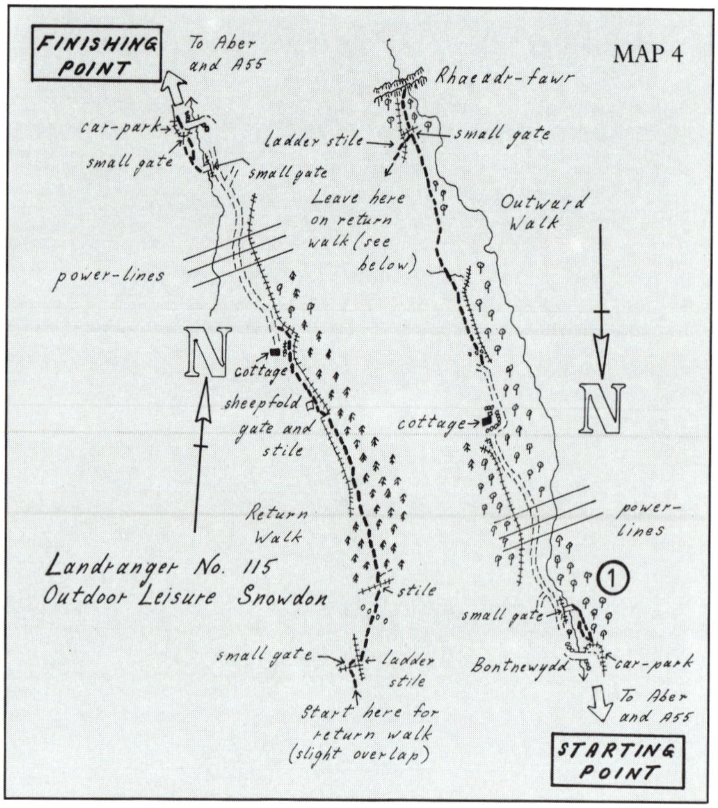

1 Coedydd Aber National Nature Reserve

The valley of the Afon Rhaeadr Fawr as far as the Aber Falls, the hilltop of Maes y Gaer and a small strip along the Afon Anafon together form the Reserve set up by the Nature Conservancy Council (see page 15) in 1975. Its main interest lies in its woodland of broad-leaved trees, mainly oak, a remnant of the great forests that once covered most of the valleys and the lower hillsides of North Wales.

Coedydd Aber Nature Trail, Nature Conservancy Council/ Forestry Commission.

Bontnewydd. The starting point for Routes 4 and 26.

1·5

Through the Gwydyr Forest

STARTING POINT
Pont-y-Pair Bridge, Betws-y-Coed (115-792567)
FINISHING POINT
Llanrwst (115-798615)
LENGTH
$2\frac{1}{2}$ miles (4 km)
ASCENT
600 ft (180 m)

Forest roads and paths through the magnificent Gwydyr Forest from Betws-y-Coed to Llanrwst with superb views over the Conwy Valley.

Route Description (Maps 5, 6)

Cross the bridge *(1)* to the north side of the river and take the L fork to go past the car-park. Follow the road up the hill and 125 yards (115 m) after the car-park, turn R down a side road. Pass the houses and where the road bends back L take a rough track half R (sign 'Forest Walks 5 and 6'). Follow this track as it rises to a higher forest road; there turn R. Go over the hilltop and immediately leave the forest road up a path to the L by some tall coniferous trees (sign 'Forest Walks 5 and 6'). This path slowly climbs the hillside, eventually reaching a stream coming down from the Aber-llyn ravine. Continue more steeply now up the ravine on a path to the L of the stream to a ruined quarry building at the top. Cross to the R in front of the building, and then L to continue in the same direction as before along a delightful path with a fence on your L, soon reaching a forest road by Llyn Parc. (Note: some tree felling has taken place in this area recently.)

Take the forest road to the R of the lake *(2)* to a crossroads, there turn R (sign 'Drws Gwyn Walk'). Follow the road round a bend and then take the L fork at a junction; at the next junction (not marked on the 1:25 000 Outdoor Leisure map) turn R (sign 'Drws Gwyn Walk'). The path descends and then bends R becoming rougher and narrower. At the bottom, turn L to continue along a level forest road *(3)*, eventually to emerge onto the hillside with superb views to the R over the green Conwy Valley with the railway bridge over the Afon Conwy below.

Further along, at a fork, take the forest road to the R and continue along the main track to reach some buildings. Just before the buildings, turn sharp R between concrete pillars and

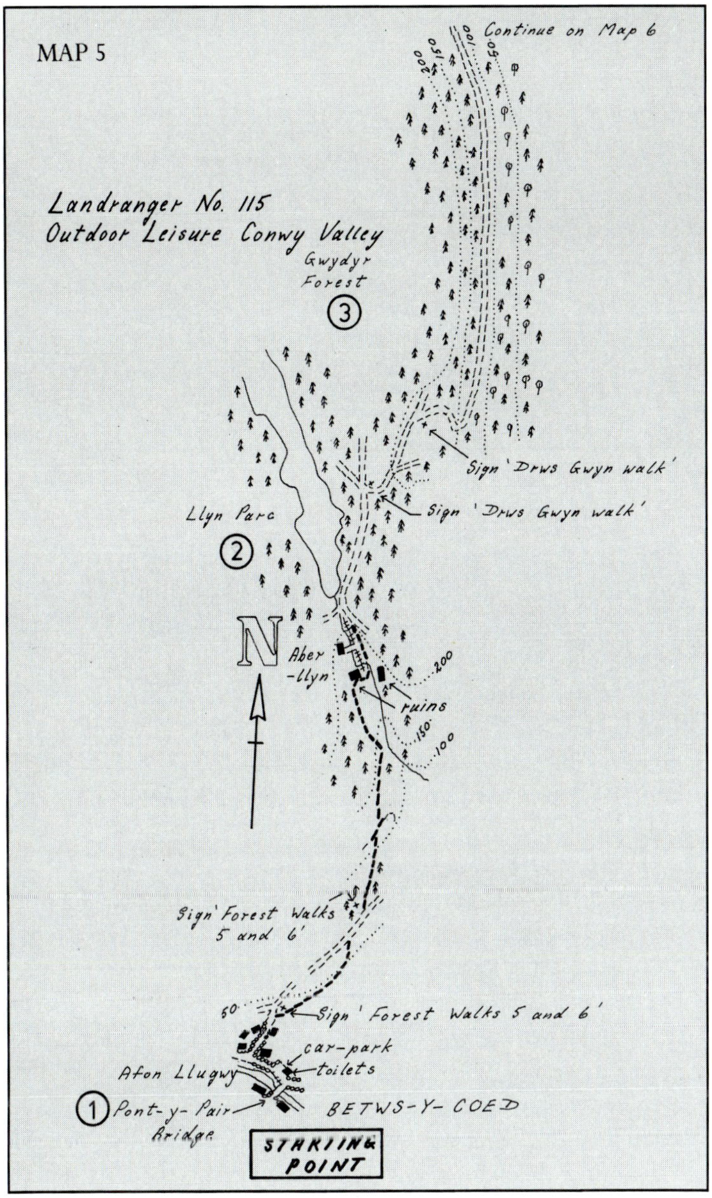

descend to a road. Here turn L for the Gwydir Uchaf Chapel *(4)* and R to descend on the road to the B5106 below. At the B5106 turn L for Gwydir Castle *(5)* and Llanrwst. In Llanrwst pass the Gorsedd stone circle *(6)* and house *(7)* at the end of Llanrwst Bridge.

1 Pont-y-Pair Bridge, Betws-y-Coed See page 32.

2 Llyn Parc

A natural lake deepened by the building of a dam to supply water to the Aber-llyn Mine which was worked in the last century for zinc and lead.

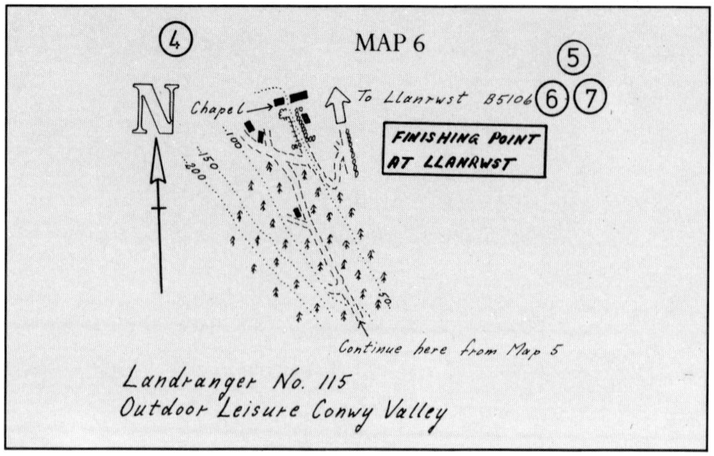

3 *The Gwydyr Forest*

6000 acres (2428 ha) of land in four blocks, three near Betws-y-Coed and the fourth south of Capel Curig, leased in 1920 by the Forestry Commission formed the nucleus of Gwydyr Forest.

Planting began in 1921 on the slopes above the Afon Llugwy and the Afon Conwy and by 1930 nearly half of the area had been afforested. The purchase of new blocks of land and afforestation continued to the early 1970s but has now ceased.

Today, the Forest occupies a total area of 14,801 acres (5990 ha), which largely consists of Sitka Spruce, Norway Spruce, Japanese Larch and Douglas Fir. About 1730 acres (700 ha) of this area is covered by broad-leaved woodland.

4 *Gwydir Uchaf Chapel*

Gwydir Uchaf means 'Upper Gwydir' and was the name given to the fine house built in 1604 by Sir John Wynn, the owner of Gwydir Castle lower down towards the river. A small private chapel was added to this in 1673 by Sir Richard Wynn; it is this which still survives, noted particularly for its painted ceiling and original gallery and pews. The Chapel is normally locked but the key can be obtained from the adjacent Forestry Commission office during normal working hours.

5 *Gwydir Castle*

This magnificently restored house on the outskirts of Llanrwst is passed on this walk. The oldest part of the building is probably a stair-tower on the south wing, which may originally have been the fortified watch-tower erected by Howell Coetmor in the early fourteenth century, but the bulk of the work was carried out in the sixteenth by Meredith ap Jevan and his son, John Wynn. It remained in the Wynn family until 1678 when it passed by marriage to the Dukes of Ancaster who held it until 1895 when it passed in turn to the Earl of Carrington. Early in this century two fires devastated a wing of the house, which, as a result, gradually became ruined. Fortunately for Gwydir Castle, however, salvation was at hand, for in 1944 the house was purchased by Arthur Clegg who, with his wife, restored the castle. This work has been continued since his death.

6 *Gorsedd stone circle, Llanrwst*

This is not of ancient origin as might be thought, but was erected in 1951 for the Proclamation Ceremony of the Royal National Eisteddfod held in that year. Other towns in Wales who have been hosts to the National Eisteddfod have similar circles.

7 *Tu-hwnt-i'r-bont*

Its name means 'The house beyond the bridge' and it is well-named for this beautiful building, now owned by the National Trust, lies at the western end of the bridge over the Afon Conwy at Llanrwst. It was built in the fifteenth century, and has been used as court house, farmhouse and toll-house. It is now open to the public both for viewing and as a restaurant from Easter to early October.

1·6

The Roman Steps

STARTING AND FINISHING POINT
Cwm Bychan (124-646314). On the A496 from Barmouth to Harlech turn R at Llanbedr (signs to Cwm Bychan) and follow the very narrow and winding road to its end at the far side of the lake.
LENGTH
3 miles (5 km)
ASCENT
925 ft (280 m)

An easy and clear path climbs slowly up from the lovely valley of Cwm Bychan, through a deciduous wood, to the famous Roman Steps, an ancient causeway of stone flags leading up the Bwlch Tyddiad. It is worth going on to the top of the col for the view to the east before returning by the same route. The route enters the Rhinog National Nature Reserve for a short distance.

Route Description (Map 7)

Leave the car-park at Cwm Bychan and turn R along the road. Opposite a barn (on the L), turn R through a gate (signs 'Roman Steps' and 'Public Footpath'). The path crosses a stone causeway

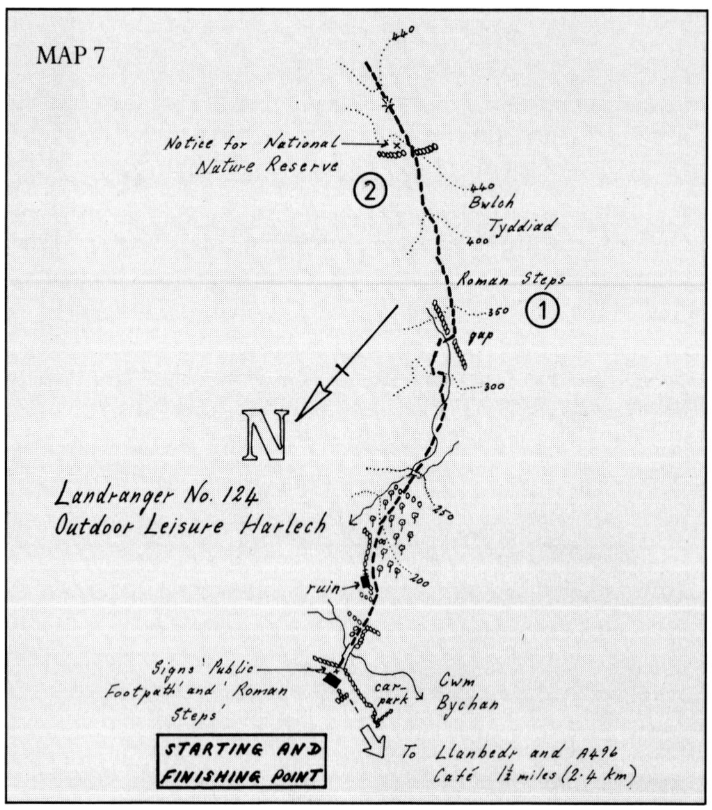

The Roman Steps, Bwlch Tyddiad

over a small stream and then continues, with a wall to the R, through a gap. Continue along this clear path, which slowly rises (there are white arrows marking the way on this section) to pass to the R of a small ruin and through a deciduous wood. Beyond the wood the paths head towards a ravine, later swinging to the R to pass through a gap in a wall. Immediately after the gap the path turns L along a particularly fine section of the Roman Steps *(1)*.

Follow the Roman Steps, slowly climbing on the R-hand side of the ravine to eventually enter the Rhinog National Nature Reserve *(2)*. Continue in the same direction on the path as far as the large cairn at the top of the pass, from which there is a magnificent view.

Return by the same route back to Cwm Bychan.

1 The Roman Steps

The paved path running from Cwm Bychan to the Bwlch Tyddiad is traditionally known as the Roman Steps, but its actual origin is obscure. Various theories place the path in the period of the Roman occupation, in Medieval times for the transport of wool from Bala to the sea at Llanbedr and

Harlech, and as late as the seventeenth century as a local path for the occupiers of the farmstead at Cwm Bychan. This section of the path is in a fine state of preservation but other sections have been identified which are now neglected.

2 *Rhinog National Nature Reserve*
An area of 991 acres (401 ha) around the Bwlch Drws Ardudwy (The Pass of the Door of Ardudwy), which includes the summit of Rhinog Fawr. A difficult area for walking with thick heather and rock, and also one of the loneliest regions in the Park.

1·7

Cwm Bychan and the Pass of Aberglaslyn

STARTING AND FINISHING POINT
Beddgelert (115-591481)
LENGTH
4½ miles (7 km)
ASCENT
725 ft (220 m)

The Pass of Aberglaslyn is one of the most beautiful spots in all Snowdonia, a magnificent ravine with rushing streams and high cliffs cloaked in trees. This route reaches the pass suddenly at the old bridge to Nantmor, which gives the best view of all. Start from Beddgelert by the Afon Glaslyn before climbing steeply up a hillside overlooking Nant Gwynant to Bwlch y Sygyn. A long descent through Cwm Bychan leads to Pont Aber Glaslyn. Return to Beddgelert through the pass along the old track of the Welsh Highland Railway. There are interesting old copper mines with tunnels, inclines, spoil heaps and aerial ropeways both before and after Bwlch y Sygyn.

Route Description (Map 8)

At the entrance to the car-park turn L down the main street of Beddgelert away from the Royal Goat Hotel. Do not cross the bridge to the L over the river, but instead continue down the minor road ahead to the R of the river. Cross the bridge at the far end and follow the river to the L past some houses to a second bridge. Again, do not cross, but go over a ladder stile and continue ahead still keeping on the R bank to cross a second ladder stile over a wall. Proceed over a marshy area, then past a barn to enter a road through a gate.

Turn R up the road and follow it for ⅝ mile (1 km) to its end at a gate just beyond the Crusader Centre. Go through the gate and take the farm road to the R, passing through a wall gap to a crossing track *(1)*. Here go R, and over a small stream to where the track bends sharp L. Do not bend with it, but instead leave and climb up the hillside ahead to a small gate. Beyond, take the clear path which inclines half L up the hillside between bushes to an upper path. Turn R and follow this path, still climbing, past a spoil heap and tunnel *(2)* and through a sharp bend to the top of the ridge (Bwlch y Sygyn).

At the top go ahead through a gap in a broken wall towards a

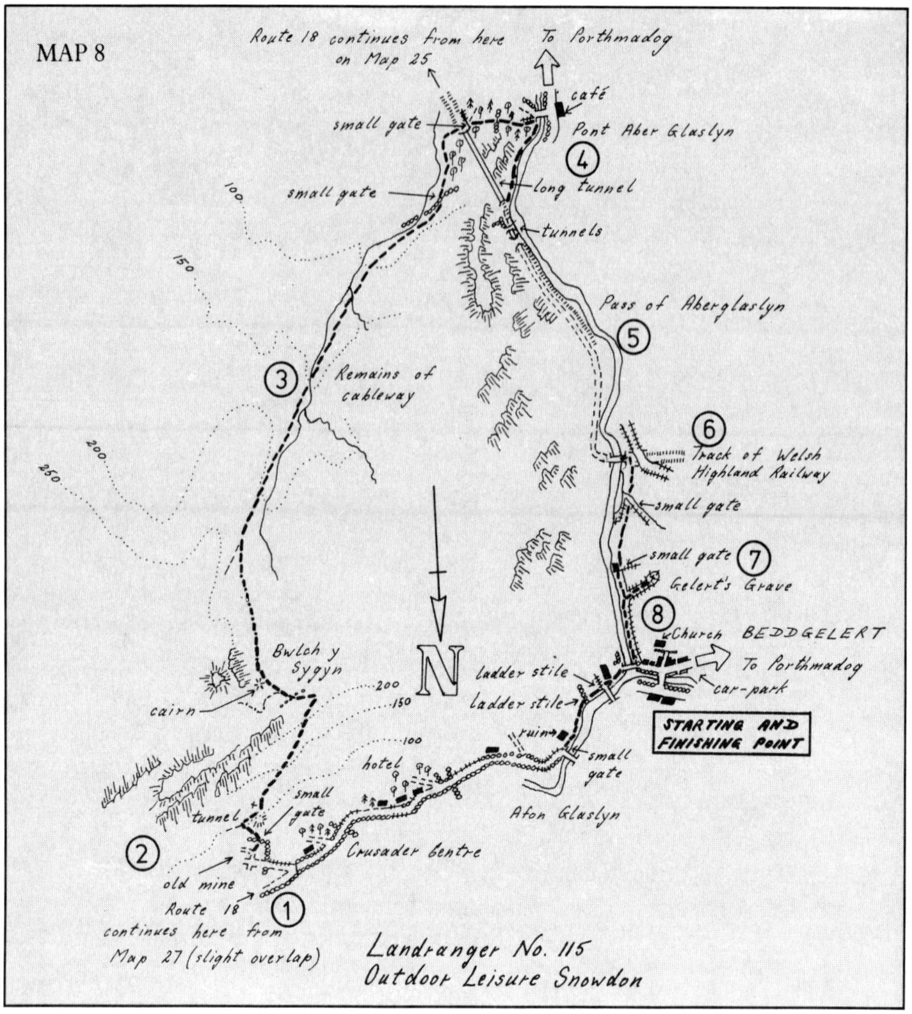

prominent rock peak. Take the faint track to the R of the peak going down a valley past a small pool. This track continues down the valley heading for a deep ravine on the L, there it joins a wider path coming in from the L. Turn R and proceed down the valley passing spoil heaps and remains of an old aerial ropeway *(2)*. The path stays near to the stream but crosses later to the R bank *(3)*. Later go through a small gate in a wall and down through a wood to reach an old railway track by a tunnel entrance.

Adventurous souls can now turn R here and cut out the corner through the long railway tunnel. More timid ones, however, should go through the small gate ahead, taking the R fork to continue through woods in the same direction to reach a bridge, Pont Aber Glaslyn *(4)*. Do not cross, but turn R and follow the path along the R bank of the river *(5)* until it rises to the old railway track *(6)* between two short tunnels (i.e. to join

Opposite *The Pass of Aberglaslyn*

up with those who have come through the tunnel). Turn L along the track crossing the river later at a bridge. Turn R after the bridge and follow a path on the L bank of the river back to Beddgelert past Gelert's Grave *(7)* and the church *(8)*.

1 Dinas Emrys
The prominent wooded hill across the A498, before Llyn Dinas is reached, has been described as the most famous Dark Age site in Wales, a place steeped in history and legend. The top of the hill is enclosed by a rampart which joins with rock outcrops to form an area of about a hectare, within which are the foundations of a Norman keep. The hilltop was probably occupied in Roman times, the ramparts being built in the post-Roman period. The greatest interest centres on a pool by the summit, the original purpose of which is now obscure.

Many legends are associated with the site. In particular, that of Vortigern, a tyrant of the fifth century, who attempted to build a castle there but was frustrated in this because of the theft of his building materials. The sacrifice of a young man, Ambros, whose blood had to be sprinkled over the hill, magicians and red and white fighting dragons are all woven into the story.

2 Copper Mines in Nant Gwynant and Cwm Bychan (see page 148)
The tunnels, spoil heaps and old buildings on the slope of the hillside above the path as you climb are the remains of the Sygyn mine where copper was mined from about 200 years ago. Another copper mine was situated in Cwm Bychan and the great wheel, towers, trucks and cables of the aerial ropeway used to carry the ore down into the valley to a crushing plant will be seen later in the walk.

3 Wangeheng
A hillside in Cwm Bychan above the village of Nantmor was the site of the Chinese city of Wangeheng used in the film, *The Inn of the Sixth Happiness,* the story of Gladys Aylward, a London parlourmaid who became a missionary in China from 1930 to 1949. North Wales was chosen because of its close resemblance to those parts of Northern China mentioned in the story. The walled city of Wangeheng was built from scaffolding covered with battens and large sheets of plasterboard. A complete Chinese village was constructed in the disused Sygyn copper mine near Beddgelert and a graveyard in the village of Llanfrothen. Many of the sturdy peasants and Japanese soldiers to be seen in the film were really local Welsh people.

Remains of copper mine, Cwm Bychan

4 *Pont Aber Glaslyn*

The shortest distance from Pont Aber Glaslyn to the sea at Porthmadog is 5–6 miles (8–9.5 km). It is surprising to learn, therefore, that in the eighteenth century Pont Aber Glaslyn lay at the head of a great shallow estuary, the Traeth Mawr, and that boats were built there for the coastal trade. The programme of land reclamation which brought about this great change came from the imagination and energy of one man, William Maddocks, who was Member of Parliament for Boston but who lived in North Wales at Dolgellau.

The western end of the Traeth Mawr was closed in 1800 by an earth embankment $1\frac{1}{4}$ miles (2 km) in length, which allowed an area of 1250 acres (500 ha) to be reclaimed into good farming land. The second stage, the sealing of the mouth of the Traeth Mawr, was a much more ambitious project, however, and took three years to complete from 1808 to 1811, the Afon Glaslyn being diverted through a channel cut into solid rock and fitted with sluice gates to control the flow.

Where the reclaimed land butted against a line of tall cliffs to the west, Maddocks planned and built a new model town, Tremadog, with market square, town hall and inns, which still looks much the same today as it did when it was built some 170 years ago. Porthmadog was begun later in 1824 with the building of a quay, but grew more rapidly in size on the prosperity of the slate trade; the slates travelling down by train from the quarries at Blaenau Ffestiniog to be unloaded into ships at Porthmadog which carried them throughout the world.

5 *The Pass of Aberglaslyn*

The Pass of Aberglaslyn gives some of the most memorable views in Snowdonia, in particular that from the old bridge, Pont Aber Glaslyn. The deep but narrow gorge has been worn out of the rock by the rushing stream, probably since the end of the Ice Age 10,000 years ago. The trees covering the slopes of the Pass were planted there during the nineteenth century, and the tunnels and broad path on its east side were part of the old line of the Welsh Highland Railway.

6 *The Welsh Highland Railway*

The three valleys of the Afon Gwyrfai, Afon Colwyn and Afon Glaslyn provide a convenient route for travellers between Caernarfon and Porthmadog via the small village of Beddgelert. Today, these valleys carry the A4085 and A498, main roads thronged each summer with tourist cars. During the early years of the twentieth century this was also the line

taken by the Welsh Highland Railway, a narrow gauge railway linking the two towns.

Inspired by the success of the Festiniog Railway, which had opened to regular passenger traffic seven years earlier, a North Wales Narrow Gauge Railways Company was incorporated in 1872 with the intention of constructing a line from Dinas near Caernarfon, where it would link up with the LNW Railway, to Rhyd-ddu about 3 miles (5 km) from Beddgelert. Work commenced in 1876 and was completed by 1881. In its early years the railway had little success, but fortunes changed dramatically when an advertising campaign coupled with an inspired re-naming of the final station from Rhyd-ddu to the more attractive South Snowdon brought a wave of prosperity to the line.

The opening of the Snowdon Mountain Railway in 1896, which took tourists to the summit instead of 3¼ miles (5 km) away, effectively killed the line however, and fortunes declined until in October 1916 the last passenger services were withdrawn.

Strangely, the line was revived in 1922 when a new company, the Welsh Highland Railway (Light Railway) Company was created with the intention of finally completing the line from Caernarfon to Porthmadog, using the facilities of the WNGRC. The older line was restored and the work on the extension completed by the summer of 1923, the final section to Porthmadog being along the old Croesor Tramway. It lasted fourteen years, passenger traffic coming to a halt in 1936 and goods traffic the following year.

The line of the old track past Beddgelert is still obvious. The line ran to the west of the village alongside the A498, before crossing the road and river to the east bank of the Afon Glaslyn at Bryn-y-Felin. The railway bridge and stone piers just south of the Royal Goat Hotel were not part of the scheme, but were built in the first years of the century as part of an earlier and eventually uncompleted line.

A Welsh Highland Railway Society was formed in 1961 with the intention of opening as much of the original line as possible and operating it with steam traction. The Society became The Welsh Highland Light Railway (1964) Ltd, three years later.

7 *The Grave of Gelert*

The inscribed stone set within a small enclosure in a field by the church at Beddgelert is said to mark the grave of the dog Gelert, after which the village is named (Bedd Gelert or Gelert's Grave). The story, heard by all who visit Beddgelert, is that Llewelyn the Great, Prince of Wales in the thirteenth century, went hunting with his followers leaving his infant son behind in the care of his dog Gelert. On his return he was horrified to find his son missing, the nursery room in disorder and Gelert covered with blood and gore. Overcome by horror, grief and anger, believing that Gelert had killed his son, Llewelyn drew his sword and slew the dog, only to discover minutes later that his son was really safe and well, buried under the cradle and that the real culprit, an enormous wolf, lay dead nearby. Presumably the wolf, intent on killing the child for food, had been killed himself by the faithful Gelert. Llewelyn, now filled with remorse, ordered that Gelert be buried in a small meadow with a monument so that the name and the story of the faithful hound should never be forgotten.

Unfortunately, the story, like so many other good stories from history, is almost certainly untrue. It is more likely that the village was named after Celert or Kelert, an early Celtic saint, and that the story of Gelert, the faithful dog, was merely the invention of several local men — in particular David Prichard of the Royal Goat Inn — who, at the end of the eighteenth century, wished to attract more visitors to this small mountain village.

8 *The Lost Monastery and Priory of Beddgelert*

The flat field to the south of the village was the site of a Celtic monastery of the sixth century and an Augustinian priory of the twelfth. The present church was part of the priory, but was extensively restored in the late nineteenth century; original features remaining are the three tall narrow windows on the east wall and the arcade with two bays on the north wall.

1·8

CWM IDWAL AND THE DEVIL'S KITCHEN

STARTING AND FINISHING POINT
Ogwen (115-649603), on the A5 from Capel Curig to Bethesda.
LENGTH
3 miles (5 km)
ASCENT
1200 ft (370 m)

ALTERNATIVE. The climb up to the Devil's Kitchen, which is the hardest part, can be avoided by traversing the slopes around the head of the lake from just past the Idwal Slabs, to meet the return path on the far side.

Cymoedd — great hollows carved out of the mountains by glaciers during the Ice Age — are a characteristic feature of North Wales. Of these, Cwm Idwal is one of the most spectacular; and fortunately also one of the most accessible, reached easily from the road at Ogwen. The route includes a steep climb up to the Devil's Kitchen and a steep, rough descent over boulders afterwards (both of which can be avoided), but otherwise the path is clear and the walking easy. The scenery throughout is superb.

ROUTE DESCRIPTION (Map 9)

Start in the car-park (Warden Centre, refreshment kiosk and toilets), beside the Youth Hostel in the minor road at Ogwen and take the path leaving from the far corner. This climbs, crossing a fence and a footbridge. Continue ahead along the footpath, which soon bends R and rises to a gate. This is the entrance to the Cwm Idwal National Nature Reserve *(1)*. Take the L-hand path around the L-hand shore of the lake. This path passes to the R of the Idwal Slabs *(2)*, then bends round to the R and climbs steeply up to the foot of the Devil's Kitchen *(3)*, which is the prominent cleft in the cliff ahead with huge boulders on the slope below.

For the return, descend down the steep slope below the Kitchen to the L of the stream, gradually leaving it towards the L. The path descends to the L shore of the lake *(4)* and follows it round back to the entrance gate of the Reserve. From the gate, follow the path down and back to your starting point at Ogwen *(5)*.

While at Ogwen, walk a few yards along the minor road to a magnificent viewpoint over the Nant Ffrancon *(6)* and the falls *(7)*.

1 Cwm Idwal

This magnificent cwm is part of the Ysbyty Estate of the National Trust, but has been leased to the Nature Conser-

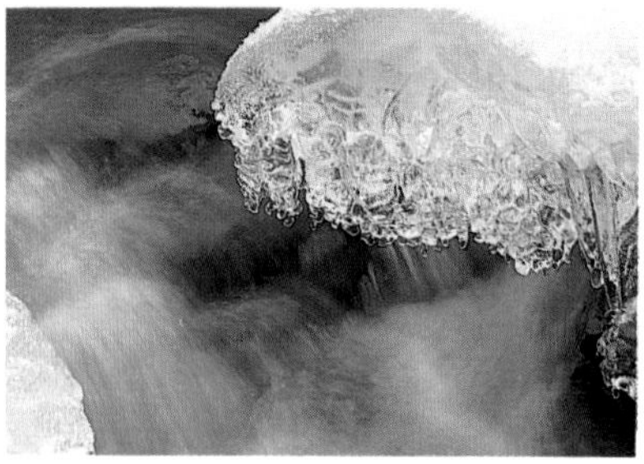

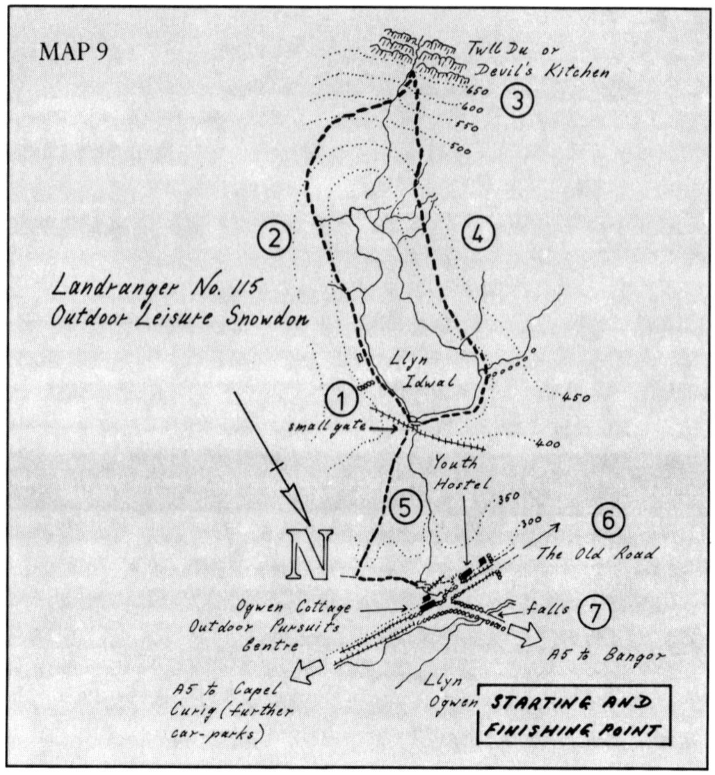

MAP 9

vancy Council. It was established as a National Nature Reserve in 1954, of considerable interest both to geologists and to botanists. Although free access is allowed, care should be taken not to disturb any rocks or plants. The small enclosures in the cwm are part of an experiment on the effects of sheep grazing and should not be entered.

Cwm Idwal National Nature Reserve Nature Trail, Nature Conservancy Council.

2 *The Idwal Slabs*

The slabs lying at an easy angle of about 50° to the horizontal to the south-east of Llyn Idwal are the famous Idwal Slabs. First climbed in 1897 by Rose and Moss, they give mainly longish climbs with small holds, but of relatively low standard because of their easy angle. They are therefore regarded primarily as a training ground for beginners. All the main rock faces hereabouts have been given names: the East and West Walls lie L and R of the slabs themselves, whilst above are Holly Tree Wall and Continuation Wall.

3 *The Devil's Kitchen*

This is the most popular name, but the Welsh name is Twll Du or the Black Hole. It is a huge chasm, deep and dark, fed by a stream coming down from a small lake on the col above.

Walkers can follow the stream down as far as a small grass

Opposite *Looking towards Foel-goch from the top of Ogwen Falls*

platform where it is possible to look down into the cleft and to Llyn Idwal below. It is also possible to scramble up the bed of the stream from below as far as the large boulder which blocks the gully. The full ascent of the Kitchen was first completed by J. M. Archer Thomson and Harold Hughes in 1895 who, using a coal hatchet borrowed from Ogwen Cottage, cut hand- and foot-holds into the frozen waterfall. The first ascent on rock was by Reade and McCulloch in 1898. The route is about 100 ft (30 m) long, of Very Difficult standard and should *not* be attempted by non-climbers.

4 *Llyn Idwal*

The low hills by the lake on the return leg are moraines left there by the glacier during the Ice Age. The lake itself has a certain sinister reputation, for legend has it that a young Prince Idwal was deliberately drowned there. For that reason, it is said, no bird will fly over the water.

5 *Llyn Ogwen*

Formed long ago on the bottom of a valley gouged out by glaciers, it is the shallowest lake of any size within the Park, being no more than about 10 ft (3 m) deep. As with all lakes in the Park, Llyn Ogwen is becoming shallower and will eventually fill up altogether due to material coming into it from the hillsides. This has already happened to the lake that once occupied the Nant Ffrancon on the opposite side of the falls.

6 *The Nant Ffrancon Pass*

The best view of the Nant Ffrancon can be obtained from the Old Road just beyond the Youth Hostel. On the left are the hanging valleys of Cwm Bual, Cwm Perfedd, Cwm Graianog and Cwm Ceunant, ahead is the Nant Ffrancon with its flat floor of green fields over which the Afon Ogwen meanders and to the right is the steep face of Penyrole-wen and of the western Carneddau. The old Penrhyn road can be seen running along the left-hand side of the valley and on the right-hand side is the present A5 which also marks the old line of Telford's Turnpike (see page 155).

7 *The Ogwen Falls (Rhaeadr Ogwen)*

Among the most spectacular in Snowdonia. View either from above or from the Old Road.

Nant Ffrancon

2·9

Conwy Mountain and the Sychnant Pass

STARTING POINT
Conwy Castle (115-784775)
FINISHING POINT
On the road from Conwy to the Sychnant Pass near Brynrhedyn (115-770775), about 1 mile (1.6 km) from Conwy.
LENGTH
6½ miles (10.5 km)
ASCENT
1475 ft (450 m)

The northern tip of the Snowdonia National Park contains two scenic gems: Conwy Mountain (Mynydd y Dref), which gives magnificent views over Conwy and the north coast of Wales, and the Sychnant Pass, which carried the old road over the high ground to the west of Conwy. This walk from Conwy links them both with a pleasant stretch up the wooded valley of the Afon Gyrach.

Route Description (Maps 10, 11)

From Castle Square in Conwy *(1) (2)*, walk down Rose Hill Street, soon bending R with it to pass through Lancaster Square and the gateway in the town wall directly ahead. Continue along the Bangor Road (A55) from the gateway, taking the second road to the L (sign 'Conwy Mountain and Sychnant Pass'). Immediately after crossing the railway bridge, turn R and walk along Cadnant Park Road following it past the cul-de-sac of Cadnant Park. After the cul-de-sac and a L bend, take the first road to the R (Mountain Road). At the end of the road at a junction, bend L (sign 'To Mountain Road') and follow the rough road up to a fork in front of some cottages (Machno Cottages). Take the R fork and pass in front of the cottages to continue along a narrow path through bushes. The path climbs steadily to the R through bracken up towards the ridge top. There are many paths around the mountain: follow the one that keeps on or close to the ridge top for magnificent views on three sides. Eventually reach the cairns on top of Conwy Mountain *(3)*.

Continue over the top to pick up a broad track; this bends down on the R of the ridge and then goes over the ridge to the L to descend to a wall. Turn R and follow the wall to its end (i.e. where it bends L) near a small pool and the junction of three paths. Take the path to the L to a fence and a cross-path. Continue along the track across heading in the same direction and descending to a farm road, there turn R and go around the

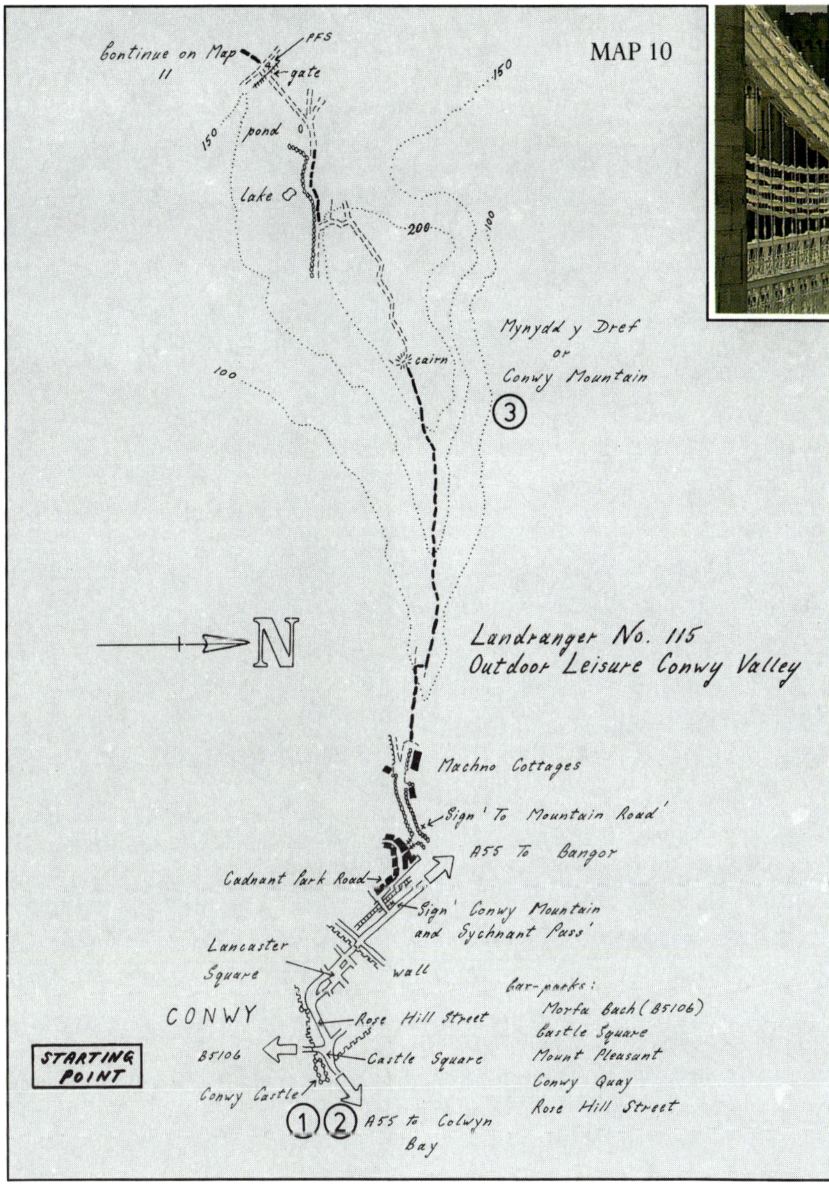

Telford's Suspension Bridge, Conwy

head of a spectacular valley (by the Sychnant Pass) *(4)*. Do not continue as far as the road ahead, but drop down some steps at the head of the valley to the R and follow a path through the valley to reach a road by some cottages. Turn L and then R at a road junction to descend to Capelulo (café and hotels).

Turn L up the minor road immediately after the Fairy Glen Hotel and follow it as far as a bridge over a stream to the L. Cross and follow the drive to a house, here turn back half L along a path which then bends R and climbs the hillside (look back as you climb for lovely views over Capelulo towards the sea). At the top, go to the L of a wall and follow it past a

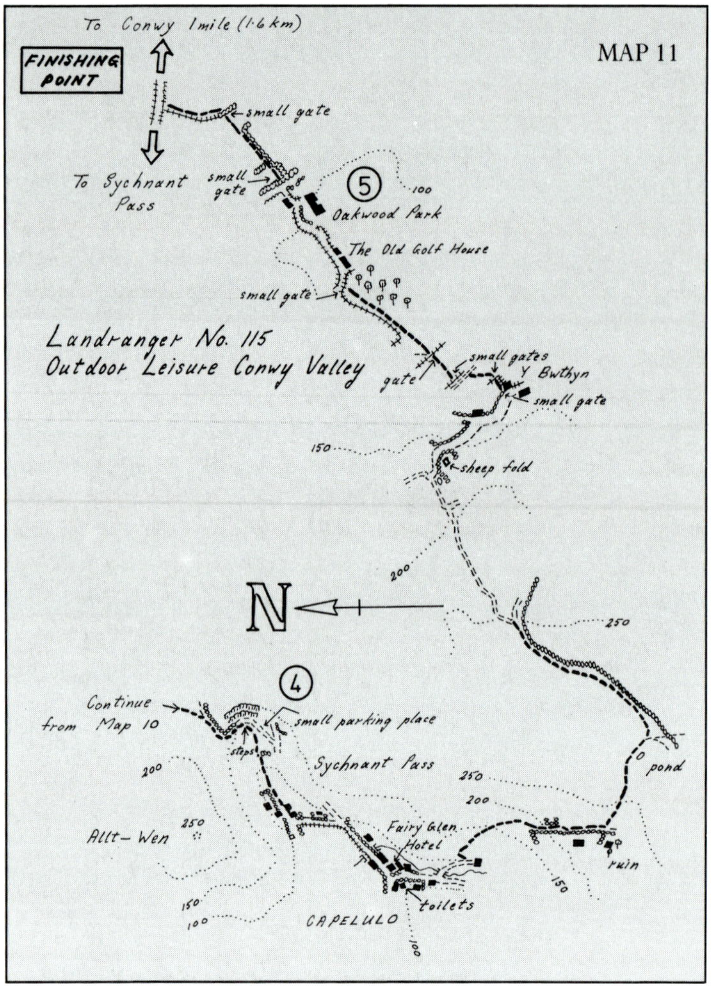

farmhouse. Go over the top into a small valley; just before a small group of trees and a ruin (over the wall to the R) turn L down a shallow valley to reach a crossing wall. Turn L and follow the wall until it bends R; just beyond the bend, go L at a path junction and to the L of a prominent hill to a T-junction by some sheepfolds. Here turn R and follow the path to a road. Turn R in the road and then L through a small gate just before the next house (Y Bwthyn).

Go past the house garage to a second small gate and then, with a fence on your R, to a third small gate. Here, go half L across a field to still another small gate and on again through a large gate; later reach a lane at the L edge of a wood by a cottage. Turn R and follow the lane to pass an exceptionally large house on the R *(5)* and then on to meet a minor road. Turn

Sychnant Pass and Conwy Mountain

R and then almost immediately L through a gate. Follow the hedge on your R to its end (i.e. where it swings R), then keep in the same direction to a small gate. Immediately after the gate turn L and go to road (PFS). Turn R and follow the road for about 1 mile (1.6 km) back to Conwy.

1 *Conwy Castle*
A Cistercian monastery holding the Charter of Llewelyn the Great and built on the site of the present parish church marked the beginning of the modern town of Conwy. But much more significant was the construction in the remarkably short time of four years between 1283 and 1287 of a great castle and fortified town on the orders of Edward I, to safeguard his recent victories over the Welsh. Since then the castle has played a part in other struggles: the rising of Owain Glyndŵr, the Wars of the Roses and the Civil War. During the summer arrange your return to Conwy after dusk, when the walls are floodlit to produce a superb spectacle.

2 *Telford's Suspension Bridge and Stephenson's Tubular Bridge*
Two famous bridges span the Conwy: the Suspension Bridge built by Thomas Telford in 1822 to carry a road and the Tubular Bridge constructed by George Stephenson in 1846–48 for the railway track. The latter is still in use, but the former was superseded by a modern bridge and is now owned by the National Trust.

3 *Castell Caer Lleion*
The summit of Conwy Mountain was the site of the Celtic hill-fort of Castell Caer Lleion probably built in the early Iron Age. The site was well chosen on a promontory with hillsides falling away steeply on all sides and high cliffs to the north, its isolated position giving it a magnificent view over the surrounding countryside. The fort occupied about 10 acres (4 ha) and was further strengthened by the building of ramparts, which are still visible.

4 *The Sychnant Pass*
The Sychnant Pass (the name means 'Dry Gorge') carried the old road from Conwy to the west thus avoiding the difficulty of forcing a road past the headland of Penmaen-bach. The road was used for this purpose until 1826.

5 *Oakwood Park*
The very large and unusual house with square tower and spire passed on the walk was originally a private house, but in its time has also served as a hotel, war-time school and hospital for mentally handicapped children.

Landscape near Dwygyfylchi

2·10

The Pony Track to Penygadair (Northern Route)

STARTING AND FINISHING POINT
Ty-nant car-park (124-698153). Leave Dolgellau along the A493 towards the toll bridge and Tywyn. Fork L on minor road. The car-park is on R after 2½ miles (4 km). There is a small information point nearby which is open in summer.
LENGTH
5 miles (8 km)
ASCENT
2400 ft (730 m)

Opposite *Cader Idris*

A short and straightforward route to the summit of Cader Idris, except for the final ascent where the path rises more steeply over rougher ground along the edge of a deep and impressive cwm with a considerable drop to the left. The track has been extensively repaired and well-marked with signs and cairns throughout, and no difficulty will be found in following it. The views, particularly from the final summit ridge, are magnificent. Return by the same route.

Route Description (Map 12)

Walk from the car-park into the road and turn R. At a telephone box (PFS) turn L over a stile and go up the farm road beyond soon passing a farm. After the farm, continue ahead through a gate, over a small bridge and uphill with a stream and wood on the L. At a footpath sign turn R, leaving the farm road through a gap, and go between two walls, soon bending L to a small gate. After the gate the path bends R over a small stream and then L uphill through a gap to a small gate in a wall. Continue up the hill moving R to a further wall with a small gate. Go through the gate and follow a path with a wall on the R.

Where the wall bends away, the path rises steeply up the ridge ahead through zig-zags, eventually passing through a gap and a stile (Rhiw Gwredydd). From the stile the path goes half L keeping near to the fence on the L. Where the fence turns to the L continue ahead up steps following a line of cairns. The path goes up the mountainside gradually approaching the lip of a great cliff dropping L into the depths of an impressive cwm, with Llyn y Gadair far below. Continue along the path on the edge of the cliff rising steeply to the summit of Penygadair.

Return by the same route back to Ty-nant.

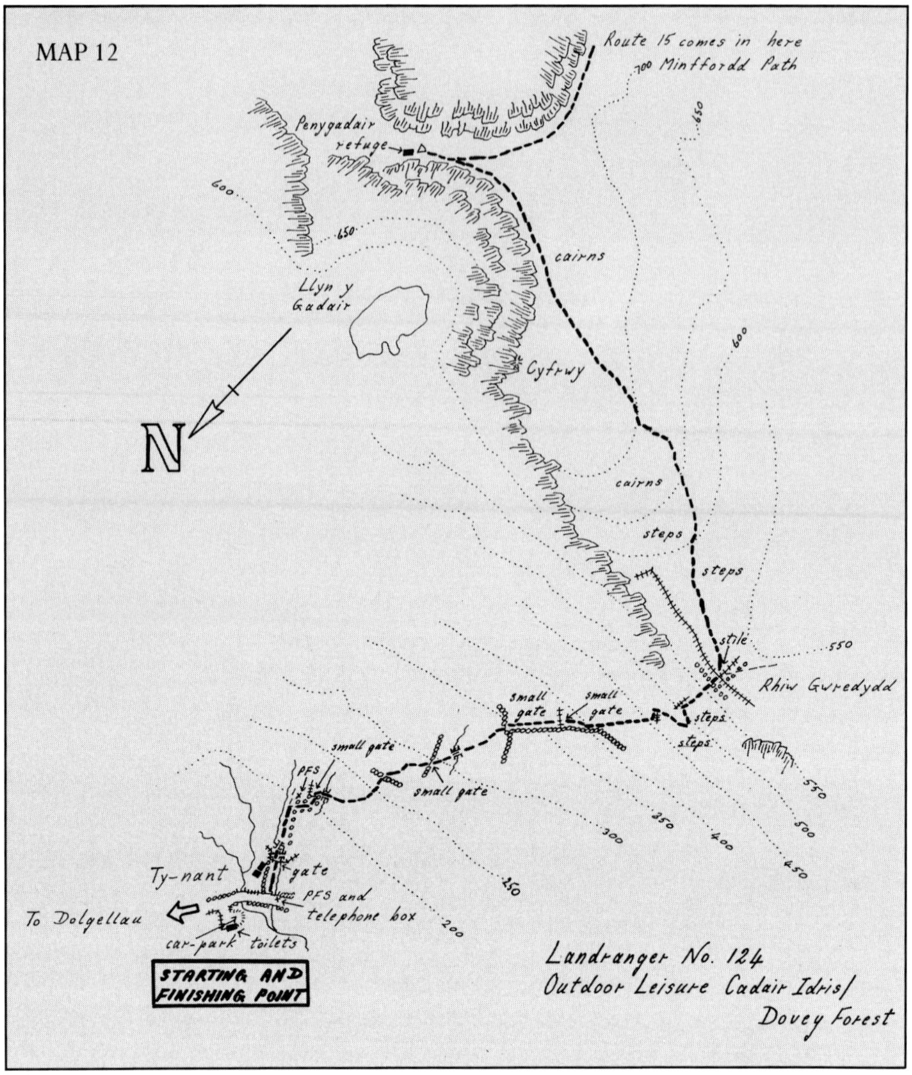
MAP 12
Route 15 comes in here
700 Minffordd Path
650
Penygadair
refuge
600
650
cairns
Llyn y Gadair
Cyfrwy
N
600
cairns
steps
steps
stile
550
Rhiw Gwredydd
small gate
small gate
steps
steps
small gate
PFS
small gate
550
500
450
400
350
300
250
200
Ty-nant
gate
PFS and telephone box
To Dolgellau
car-park
toilets
STARTING AND FINISHING POINT
Landranger No. 124
Outdoor Leisure Cadair Idris/ Dovey Forest

2·11

THE ASCENT OF RHINOG FAWR

STARTING AND FINISHING POINT
Cwm Bychan (124-646314). On the coast road (A496) from Barmouth to Harlech, turn R at Llanbedr (signs to Cwm Bychan) and follow the narrow and winding road to its end at the head of the valley.
LENGTH
$5\frac{1}{2}$ miles (9 km)
ASCENT
1825 ft (560 m)

A good and easy path leads from the lovely valley of Cwm Bychan, through a deciduous wood to the famous Roman Steps, an ancient causeway of stone flags that leads up the Bwlch Tyddiad. This is left for the ascent of Rhinog Fawr, which entails an easy scramble up scree and rock. The return can be made by the same route, but a better and much harder way is by Gloyw Lyn, which gives some very rugged walking for a mile or two.

ROUTE DESCRIPTION (Map 13)

Take Route 6 (page 46) as far as the large cairn on the pass *(1) (2)*. After enjoying the view, retrace your steps back to the wall gap and the Reserve notice. Do not go through the gap, but instead turn L and follow a narrow path as it climbs the steep and rocky hillside to the L of a wall. Where the wall ends at a small crag, the path swings L and then rejoins the wall later at a higher point. Keep with the wall to pass a lake, Llyn Du, on its R shore. Where the wall bends R at the foot of a small cliff, turn R with it over a short and low length of wall. Further along, the wall bends L around a crag; just beyond the bend take the path which leaves the wall to the L up the mountain. Climb up steep slopes with some scree to reach the summit of Rhinog Fawr.

The easiest descent is by the same route back to Cwm Bychan. A longer and more strenuous alternative, however, is the descent by the lake of Gloyw Lyn. Looking back from the OS obelisk on the summit of Rhinog Fawr go slightly L of your original direction of approach (i.e. bearing 246° magnetic) to pick up a clear path. Follow this path down over easy slopes to a large cairn and then a ladder stile over a wall (Reserve notice). Cross the stile and continue downhill on a path, eventually approaching a second wall. (The OS map shows a prominent footpath crossing here, but at the time of writing there is no sight of it.) Before the wall, turn R on bearing 17° magnetic.

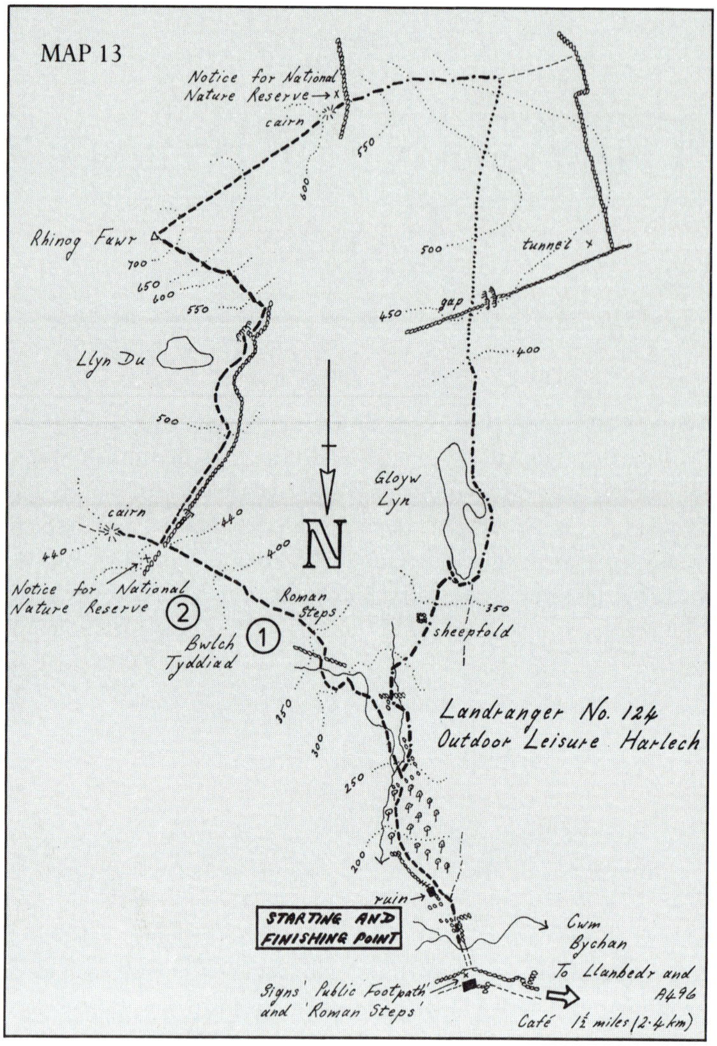

After about ½ mile (0.8 km) of hard walking over stones and heather, reach a wall and go through a gap into a small valley. Continue down the valley for a little way and then climb the ridge to the L where a path will be found that can be followed down to Gloyw Lyn. Follow the faint path to the L of the lake avoiding a marshy area. At the far end of the lake a path descends in approximately the same direction to rejoin your starting path below the wood in Cwm Bychan. Although this path from Gloyw Lyn is clear, it is not, in fact, the one shown on the Outdoor Leisure map. To find this, continue beyond the first path around the far end of the lake on a path, and at a junction take the L path to climb up a small ridge overlooking the lake. After a short distance take the faint path leading to the

Rhinog Fawr across Bwlch Drws Ardudwy

L away from the lake. Follow this path down past a sheepfold and then later through a gap in a wall to reach your starting path above the small deciduous wood.

Although all this may sound easy, in practice it isn't. For much of the way, the alternative descent described, down to and beyond Gloyw Lyn, is both hard to walk and hard to follow.

1 The Roman Steps See page 47.

2 Rhinog National Nature Reserve See page 48.

2·12

THE ASCENT OF MOEL HEBOG

STARTING AND FINISHING POINT
Beddgelert (115-589481)
LENGTH
$5\frac{1}{2}$ miles (9 km)
ASCENT
2350 ft (720 m)

Moel Hebog, the Bald Hill of the Hawk, is one of the best-known mountains in North Wales. Its ascent from Beddgelert is steep and involves some light scrambling up broken slopes of scree and rock, but the effort is well worthwhile for the top is a magnificent viewpoint. You can return by the same route, but a much better alternative is to descend down grassy slopes to the north-west to visit the cave of Owain Glyndŵr before returning by a long and interesting forest path back to Beddgelert.

ROUTE DESCRIPTION (Map 14)

Go up the small road to the R of the Royal Goat Hotel. Immediately after the hotel, turn R and go through a gate (do not turn L by the gate as indicated by the PFS), and continue to reach the old track of the Welsh Highland Railway *(1)*. Just past a small concrete tower turn L through a gate into a narrow sunken lane. Turn R along the lane and follow it as it bends L by a stream and on to a gate. Beyond, cross a bridge and turn L in a further lane. Follow this lane to the farm of Cwm Cloch.

Immediately after the barn on the R, turn R, cross a ladder stile and follow a footpath up the hill ('Walking Man' signs) to a further ladder stile by a sheepfold. Keep climbing the hill to a gap in a wall (there are cairns on both sides of the gap) and up again to a small gate in the mountain wall. Above this wall the path rises steadily, later becoming steeper and climbing over broken rocks and scree (it is clearly marked throughout with cairns). Much later, reach the ridge top by two large cairns; turn L and climb the final ridge to the summit of Moel Hebog.

Beddgelert Forest

For your return, go past the OS obelisk and continue downhill to the R of the summit wall (do not cross the ladder stile nearby). This leads down easy slopes to a col, Bwlch Meillionen *(2)*. Just after some small bends in the wall, take a faint path half R to leave the descent wall and go to a second wall running across (i.e. by cutting the corner). Turn R and follow the path

HILL & SMITH
MAKERS
BRIERLEY HILL

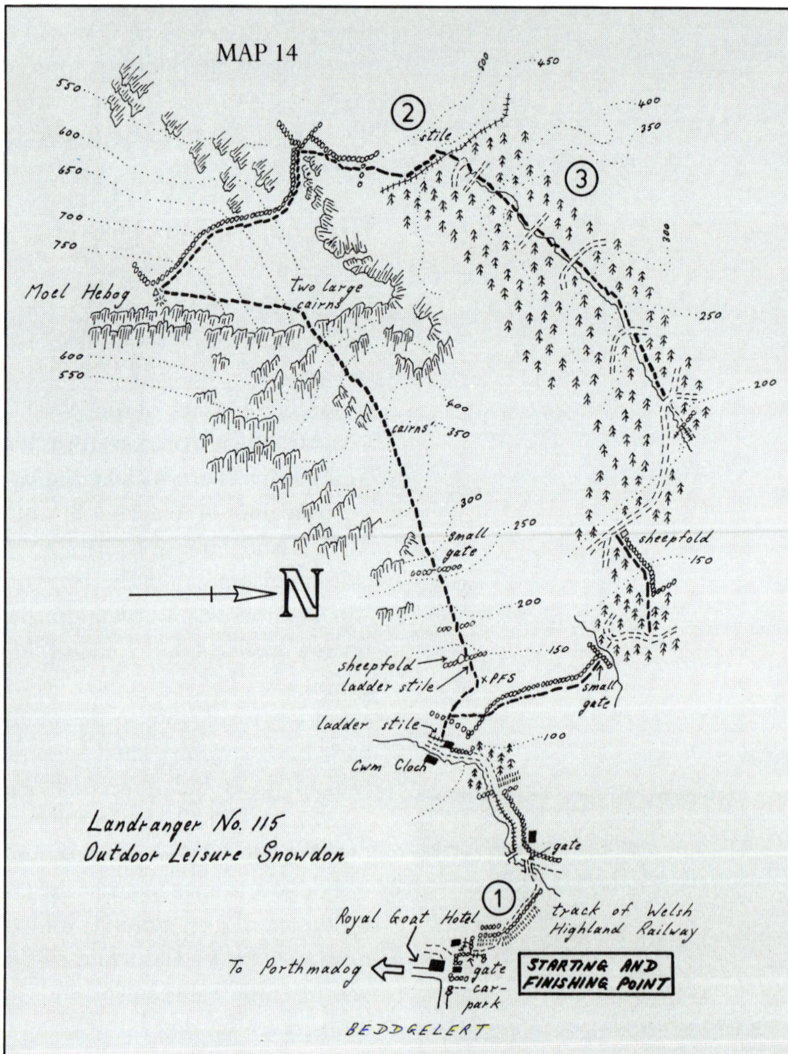
MAP 14
Moel Hebog
two large cairns
cairns
stile
small gate
sheepfold
ladder stile
PFS
Cwm Cloch
gate
sheepfold
small gate
Landranger No. 115
Outdoor Leisure Snowdon
Royal Goat Hotel
track of Welsh Highland Railway
To Porthmadog
gate
car-park
STARTING AND FINISHING POINT
BEDDGELERT
N

Approaching Cwm Cloch

down. Go through a gap and continue down to the forest below *(3)*. Turn L along the forest fence to reach a stile.

Cross into the forest and follow a path downhill across six forest roads. The path meets a small stream between the first and second forest roads and thereafter drops with it; the path is also marked throughout with red waymarks. At the sixth forest road turn R. (If you lose count of forest roads during the long descent, remember that there is a stone wall soon after the sixth and final forest road. If you do meet this, then retrace your steps back a few yards.)

Continue down to a junction. Take the L junction and immediately leave to the L down a footpath (to the R of a sheepfold). Continue down through the forest to a further forest road. Here turn R and follow it until it bends R; at this bend take a path to the L which crosses a stream and goes to a gate. Beyond, continue to the L of a wall, eventually crossing it through the second gate on the R. Continue across the field to a ladder stile by a barn. You are now back to Cwm Cloch and your way back to Beddgelert is down the lane to the L.

1 The Welsh Highland Railway

The route crosses the site of the Beddgelert station on the Welsh Highland Railway. See page 54.

2 Ogof Owain Glyndŵr

The peak of Moel yr Ogof has a number of horizontal clefts on its eastern face. The largest of these is said to be the hiding place of Owain Glyndŵr (Owen Glendower) when pursued by the English.

Wales had remained an independent kingdom until the middle thirteenth century despite numerous attempts to subdue it. In several years (1282–84) of ruthless warfare, however, Edward I overran Wales and built a series of powerful castles at Conwy, Harlech and elsewhere to safeguard his conquests. Despite serious revolts in 1287 and 1294 the Welsh generally accepted the rule of the English and were gradually absorbed both into the administration of Wales and into the English armies in their wars against France and Scotland. In 1400, however, a more serious revolt began under Owain Glyndŵr, a man raised as an English gentleman, but who had from his ancestry the strongest claim for the title of Prince of Wales. Within a few years the revolt had spread throughout Wales, the great castles of Aberystwyth and Harlech had fallen and an independent government had been formed supported by an alliance with the French.

By 1410, however, the tide had turned, the castles had been re-taken and Owain Glyndŵr had become a hunted fugitive. We hear of him in 1415 and then no more.

The cave can be reached from the top of the forest.

3 The Beddgelert Forest

Beddgelert Forest is part of the Snowdonia National Forest Park. There is a Forestry Commission campsite within the Forest, a wayfaring course and several forest walks.

Moel Hebog

2·13

The Traverse of the Glyder Ridge

STARTING AND FINISHING POINT
Ogwen (115-649603), on the A5 from Capel Curig to Bethesda.
LENGTH
$5\frac{1}{2}$ miles (9 km)
ASCENT
2375 ft (720 m)

The great ridge of Glyder Fach and Glyder Fawr is reached from Ogwen by a path that ascends near the outfall of Llyn Bochlwyd before striking over to the wild col of Bwlch Tryfan. The final ascent to the summit ridge is across and up steep scree. The summits themselves, with their huge and weird towers of weathered rock, are the most unusual in Snowdonia. The return to Ogwen is down exceptionally steep scree slopes to the west of the Fawr, followed by a spectacular descent to the foot of the Devil's Kitchen. A short route, but one of the finest mountain expeditions in Snowdonia for the moderate walker.

Route Description (Maps 15, 16)

Start in the car-park by the Youth Hostel at Ogwen. Leave the car-park along a well-maintained path from the far corner; this crosses a fence and a footbridge and rises up the hillside. Where the path bends R, do not turn with it but continue in the same direction as before along a faint path, heading for some waterfalls, the Bochlwyd Falls, which can be seen on the hillside ahead. Work has been done on this path recently which climbs on the R-hand side of the falls. At the top, cross over to the opposite bank and continue on the path around the L shore of a lake, Llyn Bochlwyd. The path then rises and bends to the L to reach the Bwlch Tryfan, a magnificent col between Tryfan and Glyder Fach.

Cross the wall by one of the ladder stiles and turn R to climb up the steep hillside. The path climbs up the scree to the L of the rocks ahead (Bristly Ridge), to reach the top. (Route 25 joins here.) Continue across the top to the prominent pile of huge slabs ahead *(1)*. Further along, reach the summit of Glyder Fach, which is the second pile of slabs, and further still the weird spires of rock, which are known as the Castle of the Winds.

Do not attempt to pass this on the R-hand side where there is a considerable drop, use instead a path that descends on the L

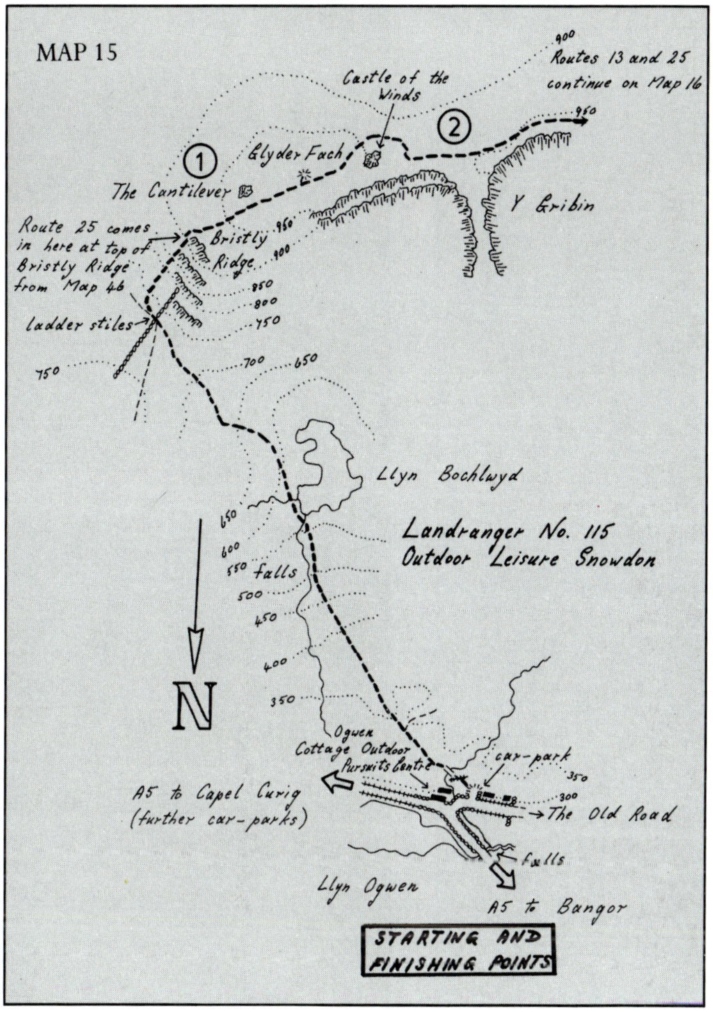

and then rises again beyond. The path from here to Glyder Fawr *(2) (3) (4)*, slightly to the L of the ridge top, is very clear and well-marked with cairns. The prominent pile of rocks at the far end marks the summit. The path continues in the same direction for a short distance beyond the summit, before turning to the R and dropping down very steep scree well-marked with cairns. Continue down to the grassy col by Llyn y Cŵn.

When you reach the grassy slopes of the col from the scree, turn sharp R to cross an area of marshy ground past a prominent cairn to pick up a path. Follow this path down a small valley, well-marked with cairns, eventually meeting a small stream. *Do not follow the stream down as it goes over a considerable cliff.* Instead, bend to the L down a shelf following the base of the cliff, to the bottom of the Devil's Kitchen *(5)*. Cross the stream at the base of the Kitchen and descend the boulder slope on the L-hand side, eventually reaching a path that will lead you around the L-

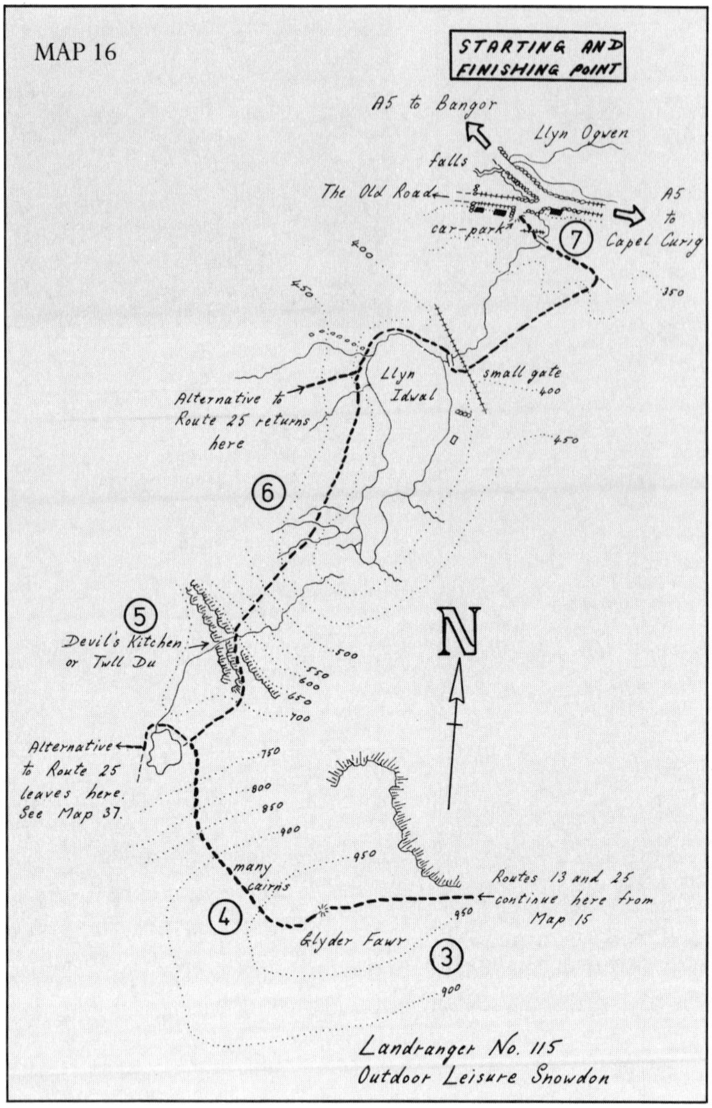

hand side of Llyn Idwal *(6)*. At the far end of the lake cross a footbridge and go through a gate in a fence; then follow the clear path beyond down to Ogwen *(7)*.

1 The Cantilever

The huge horizontal slab of rock about 25 ft (7.5 m) long, with at least 9 ft (2.7 m) projecting into space, a short distance north of the summit of Glyder Fach, is known as the Cantilever. It is one of the most photographed sights in Snowdonia. Thomas Pennant, who visited North Wales in

Bristly Ridge, Glyder Fach

1778, included a drawing of the Cantilever in his book *Tour of Wales*, looking remarkably the same as it does today. It is highly likely that walkers two centuries hence will find it still in place.

2 *Dyffryn Mymbyr*

The farm of Dyffryn Mymbyr, situated roughly mid-way between Capel Curig and the Pen-y-Gwryd by the Llynnau Mymbyr, was the scene of Thomas Firbank's best-selling book *I Bought a Mountain*. Firbank was a Canadian by birth, but had been educated in England and had spent his holidays on a farm in Merionethshire. In 1931 he returned to England and bought a sheep farm of 2400 acres (970 ha) with its stock of 1300 sheep, where he stayed until the war came in 1939. *I Bought a Mountain* is the story of his eight years on the Welsh hill-farm. The mountainside of Glyder Fach was part of the farm, hence the title.

The book, first published in 1940, was an immediate best-seller and still sells well today; it is usually on sale in shops within the Park.

3 *The Marching Camp at Pen-y-Gwryd*

By AD 74, some thirty years after the Romans had landed upon the British shore at Richborough in Kent, the frontier of the Roman Empire had been pushed to a line corresponding roughly to that of modern Wales. Three great legionary fortresses had been built at Chester, Wroxeter and Caerleon, but it is unlikely that the frontier was ever wholly peaceful, and campaigns against the Welsh tribes were mounted by Scapula between AD 47 and 52, by Veranius in 57 and by Paulinus in 58 and 59. The final conquest was not achieved however until AD 75 when Frontinus defeated the tribe of the Silures in South Wales and AD 78 when Agricola conquered the Ordovices of North Wales. But from then onwards for 400 years Wales was an integral part of the Roman Empire.

The main line of advance of the Roman army probably took place over high ground, as the river valleys would be covered by dense forest and difficult to negotiate. When the invading army stopped it would erect a temporary camp, now referred to as a marching camp. Here the legionnaires would throw up an earth wall, 5–6 ft high (1.5–1.8 m), upon which they would erect a palisade of stakes to give greater protection. Inside, tents of leather would be laid out in regular order.

The valley and slopes to the left of the Glyder Ridge mark one of the lines of advance of the Roman Army, and by the Pen-y-Gwryd Hotel is the site of a marching camp, the only one known in North Wales at the present time.

Glyder Fawr

4 *The Pen-y-Gwryd Hotel*
This famous hotel stands at the junction of the roads to Llanberis, Capel Curig and Beddgelert about 1 mile (1.6 km) from Pen-y-Pass. Originally a farmhouse owned by John Roberts of Llanberis, it became an inn when Henry Owen decided to take out a licence in 1847, and with his wife, Ann, was to stay there as landlord for forty-four years until his death in 1891. In his time the inn grew in importance and became the Home of Mountaineering in North Wales. It declined somewhat after about 1900 due to the influence of Owen Rawson Owen at the Gorphwysfa, but since 1947 it has resumed its original standing and is today one of the great centres of British mountaineering.

Pen-y-Gwryd has always been a base for Everest expeditions and in 1953 the team for the successful expedition stayed there for part of their training. The Everest Room at the hotel carries on its ceiling the signatures of members of the expedition, and in the residents' private room there is a case containing souvenirs of the expedition including samples of rock from the summit and a length of the rope which linked Hilary and Tensing during their final climb. Since 1953, a reunion of expedition members has been held every five years at the Pen-y-Gwryd.

5 *The Devil's Kitchen*
A magnificent view down into the Kitchen can be obtained by following the outflow from Llyn y Cŵn as far as a small grassy platform above the cleft. Afterwards, retrace your steps back to Llyn y Cŵn to continue the descent as described. (See page 58.)

6 *Llyn Idwal* See page 60.

7 *Ogwen*
Do not leave Ogwen without a visit to the falls and a short walk down the Old Road for a superb view of the Nant Ffrancon Pass. (See page 60.)

View from the Miners' Track near Glyder Fach (the Pen-y-Gwryd Hotel is left of centre at the junction of the three roads)

2·14

The Ascent of Moel Siabod

STARTING AND FINISHING POINT
Plas y Brenin, near Capel Curig (115-716578). Plas y Brenin is the very large building on the L about 550 yd (500 m) from Capel Curig along the road (A4086) to Llanberis and Beddgelert.
LENGTH
$6\frac{1}{2}$ miles (10.5 km)
ASCENT
2225 ft (680 m)

From Plas y Brenin, forest roads and paths run through beautiful woods by the Afon Llugwy to reach the old bridge of Pont Cyfyng. From there, a long gradual climb leads up the eastern flank of Moel Siabod to reach the ridge of Daiar Ddu above Llyn y Foel. The Daiar Ddu gives a long but easy scramble, finishing at the summit cairn. The summit ridge is traversed, followed by a descent over grassy slopes to the coniferous forests above Plas y Brenin. The view from the footbridge at Plas y Brenin towards the Snowdon Horseshoe is considered one of the finest in Snowdonia.

Route Description (Maps 17, 18)

Go through a small gate (PFS) to the R of the main building of Plas y Brenin *(1)* and descend to a footbridge. Immediately after the footbridge, turn L along a forest road which runs along the R-hand side of a small lake. Keep along this forest road passing a house on the L and another forest road coming in from the R. Take a second forest road to the R just afterwards and follow it to its end at some steps, where a path continues in the same direction. Follow this path to a footbridge. Do not cross, but instead turn R and keep along the R bank of the river passing over a ladder stile and then through a gate. Beyond go to the L of a small barn, then head slightly R for a gap in a fence at the front of a farmhouse. Go through the gap, over a small stream and up to the house wall, there turn L. Rise to a gate which leads into a minor road and turn R.

Follow the road, turning R at a junction after 100 yards (90 m), until it ends at the farm of Rhôs; there continue on the rough road beyond to a ladder stile by an old house and then on again to a second ladder stile in a fence *(2)*. Higher still, take the L fork at a junction and, crossing a third ladder stile, continue to a lake. Follow the clear path to the R of the lake and then up to some slate quarries ahead *(3)*. Go past the spoil heaps and

Opposite *The Snowdon Horseshoe from the Llynnau Mymbyr*

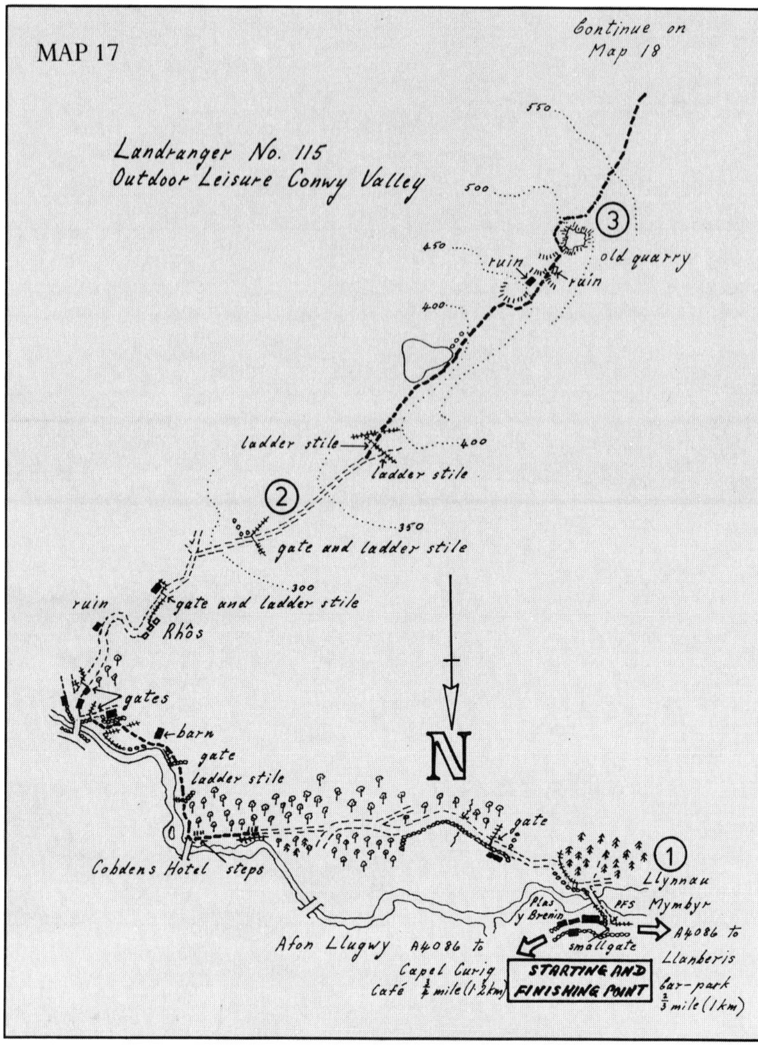

ruined buildings of the quarry and on to the L of a deep sinister pit filled with black water into which the water cascades on the far side. The path continues beyond the pit up the valley to reach the top of a ridge from which a second lake can be seen. Keep on the path to pass this lake also on its R side and continue on to a further ridge ahead (there is a splendid view from here of the Lledr Valley) *(4)*. Turn R and climb up the ridge following a path and cairns to the OS obelisk on the summit of Moel Siabod.

For the return, turn R from your approach route along the rocky summit ridge to the far end and drop down to the start of the grassy slopes of the mountain, here turn half L leading downhill (aim for the R-hand end of the lake in the valley). There is no path at first, but later you should be able to pick up a path marked with cairns; follow it down to a ladder stile in a

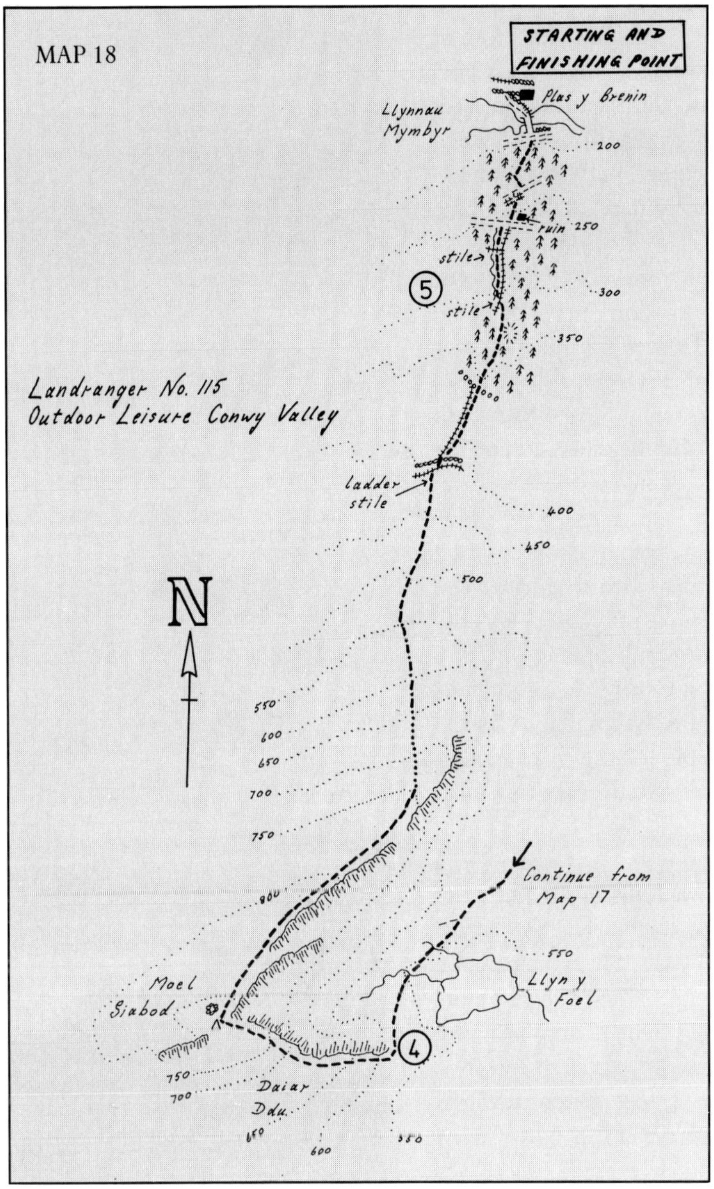

fence. Cross and continue to descend on a rough path, with a fence on the L, to a forest *(5)*. Continue to follow the path down through the forest to a stile in a fence and then later to meet a forest road. Cross half R to go on a path to the L of a small ruined hut, and then down a particularly delightful stretch of path under trees. At a crossing track turn R, then immediately L and down again to reach the bridge by Plas y Brenin.

1 Plas y Brenin (The King's House)
The Old Road up the Nant Ffrancon Pass was constructed by Richard Pennant – owner of the great quarry at Bethesda – to

connect his lands at Bethesda and near Bangor with those at Capel Curig. At the latter place he built an inn, the Capel Curig Inn, in 1800–1801 to serve the tourist trade. In later years, 1808–1848, it also served the Royal Mail Coach which carried the Irish Mail up the new turnpike between Shrewsbury and Holyhead. George Borrow, author of *Wild Wales*, visited the inn in 1854 on a day's walk from Cerrig-y-Drudion to Bangor and found it '... a very magnificent edifice ... from whose garden Snowdon may be seen towering in majesty at the distance of about six miles'. Other visitors over the years included Queen Victoria, Edward VIII, Sir Walter Scott, Queen Mary, George V and Lord Byron. In 1870–71 – no doubt as a result of this heavy visitation by royalty – the name of the inn was changed to the Royal Hotel.

During World War II, the inn was taken over as a training centre for mountain warfare, but returned to its former use afterwards. In 1954, however, it was purchased by the Central Council for Physical Recreation and opened in 1955 as The Snowdonia National Recreation Centre. In a reorganization during the early 1970s the CCPR was replaced by the Sports Council, who became responsible for the management of the Centre. It is now called Plas y Brenin, The National Centre for Mountain Activities.

2 *Bryn-y-Gefeiliau*

The conquest of the Ordovices in Snowdonia in AD 78 by the Roman Army under Agricola marked the end of active campaigning in Wales; their control over a vanquished foe was then assured by a series of forts placed at strategic points and joined together by roads, along which supplies and reinforcements could be speedily passed. One such fort was built about 1½ miles (2.4 km) from Capel Curig towards Betws-y-Coed, where the great Roman road of Sarn Helen from Carmarthen to the Conwy Valley crossed the River Llugwy. It was built early in the second century and formed a permanent base for an auxiliary unit of perhaps 500 or 1000 men. The site can be seen from about the second ladder stile on the climb up to Moel Siabod, it is to the R of the camp site (brightly coloured tents) in the valley behind you.

3 *The Capel Curig Slate Quarry Company*

The deep and awesome pit, by the path to Moel Siabod was worked by the Capel Curig Slate Quarry Company from the nineteenth century. The company was amalgamated with

View from the footbridge behind Plas y Brenin

several others in 1918 to form the Caernarvonshire Crown Slate Quarries Company but, like most other slate quarries in the area, closed down later.

4 *Dolwyddelan Castle*

From the bottom of the ridge beyond Llyn y Foel and before the final climb to the summit of Moel Siabod there is a splendid view of the Lledr valley ahead and half left. The prominent castle, perched on the edge of a rocky crag which falls steeply into the valley below, is Dolwyddelan. Built by a Prince of Gwynedd in the thirteenth century, it was reconstructed later in the same century by Edward I as part of his massive programme of castle building. The present remains consist of the rectangular keep to the east, the smaller West Tower, ditches and part of the curtain-wall.

5 *The Gwydyr Forest*

The forest behind Plas y Brenin is part of the Gwydyr Forest acquired by the Forestry Commission in 1920. The plantings have been of conifers, but there is a belt of natural oak to the north of the forest towards Capel Curig.

2·15

THE TRAVERSE OF CADER IDRIS

STARTING POINT
Double iron gates ('Idris Ltd' on each) on B4405 about 450 yd (410 m) from its junction with A487 (124-730113). There is now a car-parking area between the gates and the junction.
FINISHING POINT
Car-park at Ty-nant (124-698153)
LENGTH
6 miles (9.5 km)
ASCENT
2900 ft (880 m)

Cader Idris is one of the most popular mountains in Snowdonia, most people climbing it by the Pony Track from the Dolgellau side. The Minffordd Path from the south, however, is far better, reaching the summit by a long ridge that gives grand views to the left over the Tal-y-llyn Valley and to the right down high cliffs into the magnificent Cwm Cau. Even better than that is a traverse of the mountain, using both routes with a diversion to the summit of Cyfrwy.

ROUTE DESCRIPTION (Maps 19, 12 — see also page 70)

(1) Go through a small gate by the large double gates (PFS and Park Information Board), up an old drive between bushes and over a footbridge. Beyond the stream, continue up the drive to a small gate in a fence — this is the entrance to the Cader Idris National Nature Reserve *(2)*. Then follow a path which rises steeply up through a wood; here, a river to the R of the path falls in a magnificent series of white cascades. At a small stream coming across to join the main stream, the path bends L and then R over the stream to resume the same direction as before. Pass through a small gate in a wall and continue rising along a path leaving the wood behind. The path goes up the hillside, at first with the stream still to the R, but later swinging L gradually leaving it. Go past two Reserve enclosures and on up the valley towards the small ridge ahead.

Eventually, reach a large cairn where the path forks. Take the L-hand path which rises steeply uphill (cairns) to reach the crest of a higher ridge. As you climb, Llyn Cau becomes visible down to the R. Continue to follow the path that goes up the ridge to the R, well-marked with cairns, with good views on both sides. Later reach a fence at the summit of Craig Cau, and continue across the top to drop down to Bwlch Cau. There is a considerable cliff to the R throughout this section and care is necessary, particularly in windy conditions, if you keep near to

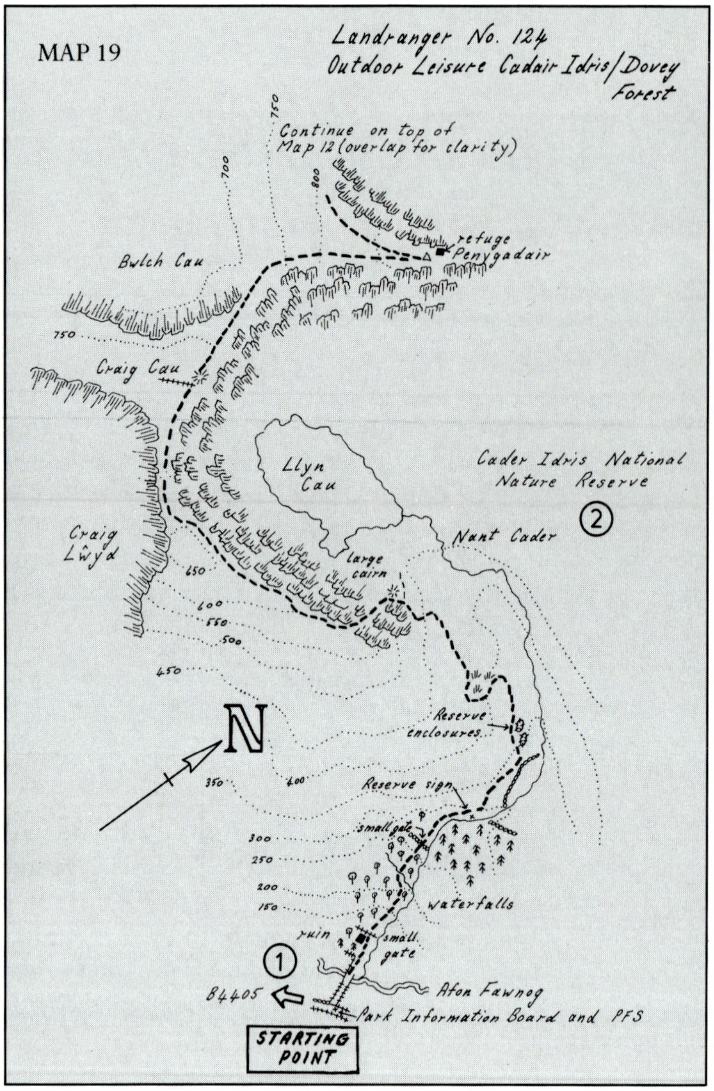

the edge for the excellent views. From Bwlch Cau, ascend on a path following cairns to the OS obelisk on the summit of Cader Idris.

From the summit, looking back on your approach route, descend slightly R of your approach route on a path with a crag to the R. The path keeps near to the cliff edge for some way, then swings L and away from the edge; where the path swings away leave the path and climb keeping to the L of the cliff edge to the summit of Cyfrwy. Leave the summit SW to pick up the path again lower down the mountainside. The path descends steadily to meet a fence (on your R) and then on to a wall corner.

Cader Idris seen from across Afon Mawddach

Here, cross a stile to the R by a gate and then pass through a gap in a broken wall beyond to continue the descent. Go through zig-zags and down on a clear path to a wall, there turn R and follow the wall to a small gate (a fence is crossed along the way). After the gate, the path bends L, goes through a gate and then a wall gap. Lower down still it swings R to a further small gate. Go through this gate and along a path between two walls into a lane, there turn L. Follow the lane over a bridge and through gates to reach a road. Turn R and walk the short distance to a car-park (if some kind person is waiting for you) or continue about 3 miles (5 km) to Dolgellau (if not).

1 *The Bala Fault and the Tal-y-llyn Valley*

The straight line and the steep sides of the Tal-y-llyn Valley make it one of the most impressive sights in North Wales. It is the result of a combination of forces: movements in the earth's crust, river erosion and glacial action.

Movements in the earth's crust can produce enormous forces of compression and tension which may, over long periods of time, result in extensive folding of the surface layers. In some cases the forces involved are so great that faults are formed — miles in length and thousands of feet deep — along which an immense thrusting action occurs with a relative displacement of the rocks on the opposite sides.

The valleys from Bala to Tywyn mark the line of such a fault, usually called the Bala Fault. In this case, the rocks on the south side have been displaced about 2 miles (3.2 km) from those on the north side. The rock along the fault line was mudstone, a soft, weak and easily eroded rock, which would have been extensively shattered during the progress of the faulting. This line of soft and shattered rock was rapidly worn away by river action to produce a deep and steep-sided valley. Finally, the river valley itself was deepened and straightened further by glacial action during the Ice Age; the lake of Tal-y-llyn probably forming later in a hollow in the valley gouged out by the ice. An excellent view of the valley is obtained as you come south-west down the A487 from the Cross Foxes Inn.

2 *Cader Idris National Nature Reserve*

A substantial part of Cader Idris from the Tal-y-llyn Valley to the summit ridge between Penygadair and Mynydd Moel, including Llyn Cau, has been designated as a National Nature Reserve (see page 16). The main attractions are the oak woodland, typical of the forests that once covered most of the valleys and low hillsides of Wales, and the superb Cwm Cau, which shows the usual characteristics of glaciation.

Opposite *Approach to Cader Idris from Minffordd Path*

2·16

THE EASTERN CARNEDDAU

STARTING AND FINISHING POINT
Capel Curig (115-721581)
LENGTH
9 miles (14 km)
ASCENT
2000 ft (610 m)

An excellent walk with superb views along two contrasting valleys: the beautiful wooded valley of Llyn Crafnant and the long, barren and lonely valley of Llyn Cowlyd.

ROUTE DESCRIPTION (Maps 20–23)

Leave Capel Curig over a stile (PFS) to the L of the war memorial and church (i.e. on the opposite side of the A5 road from the Post Office) and follow a path which goes uphill inclining slightly L. At the top of the field go through a gap in the wall to the R of the top L-hand corner and immediately turn L over a small stream and then R to resume your original direction (ignore two tracks to the L after the stream). Continue through a shallow valley between a prominent rock spire and a hillside. Enter a wood over a stile and follow a path through it to leave at the far end by a gate. The path goes ahead to a gap in a wall and then on to a small bridge over a stream. After the bridge, bear slightly L (i.e. on the L-hand path) gradually leaving the stream through a shallow valley to the R of a small hill. Go through a gap in a fence and continue with the fence on the L; soon the path bends L with the fence to a gate. After the gate, the path bends R and follows a stream, gradually climbing to a col. On the col, continue ahead, dropping sharply down into the valley ahead through a narrow gully. There is now a superb view ahead over Llyn Crafnant with the long ridge of Creigiau Gleision to its L.

Descend the steep hillside on the path through wall gaps to reach a wall, there turn R and walk down by the wall. After a short distance go L through a gate and head towards the farm ahead (Blaen-y-nant). Turn R immediately after the farmhouse along a farm road; where the farm road bends R, go L on a grassy track to meet a second farm road by a small cottage (Tan-y-Manod). Turn L and follow the farm road to a gate at a second farm (Hendre). Immediately after the gate, turn R over a stile

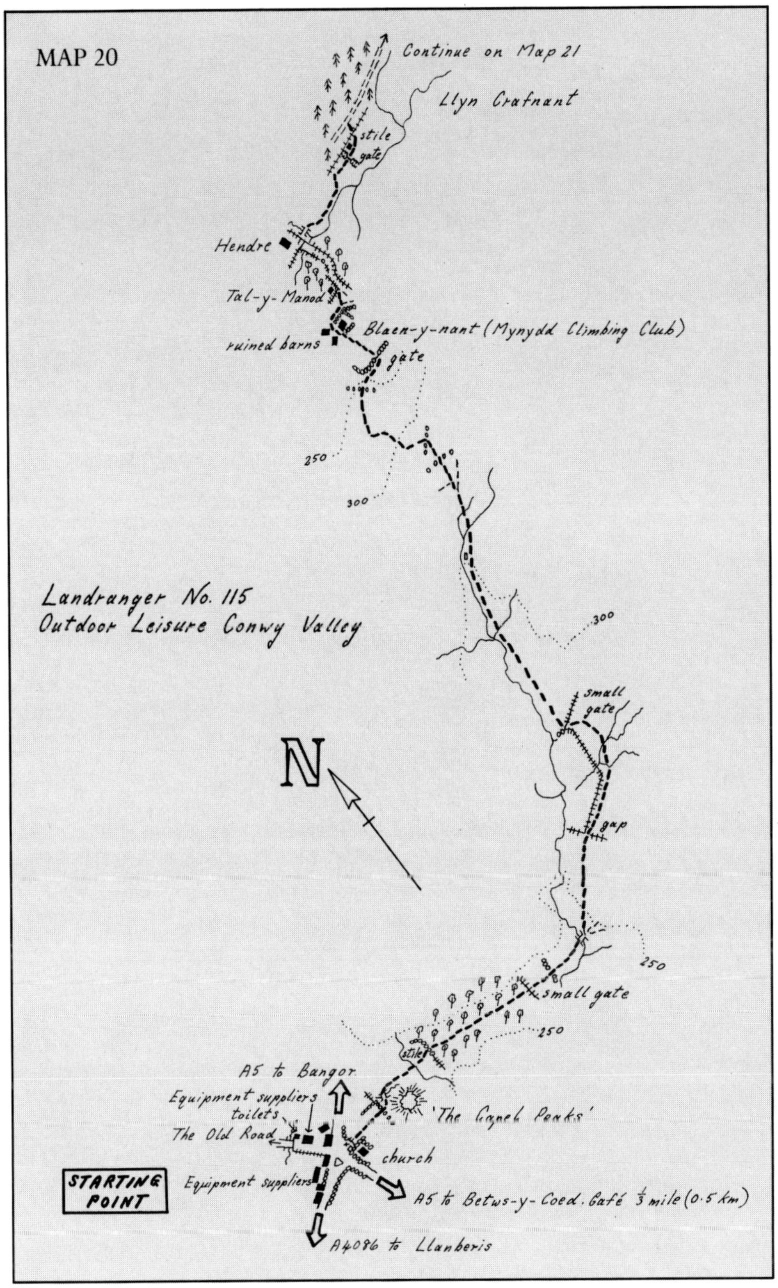

and a small bridge (PFS) and go ahead to reach a stream, then continue on its L bank. Where the stream bends R, leave the bank and go L towards a wood. Go through a gate and further along, enter the wood by a stile just beyond a ruined hut. Inside the wood, reach a forest road and turn R. Follow this road, with the lake on the R, to the far end of the lake; there turn R over a bridge to reach a road *(1)*.

Turn L. After 1½ miles (2.4 km) pass the entrance to a house,

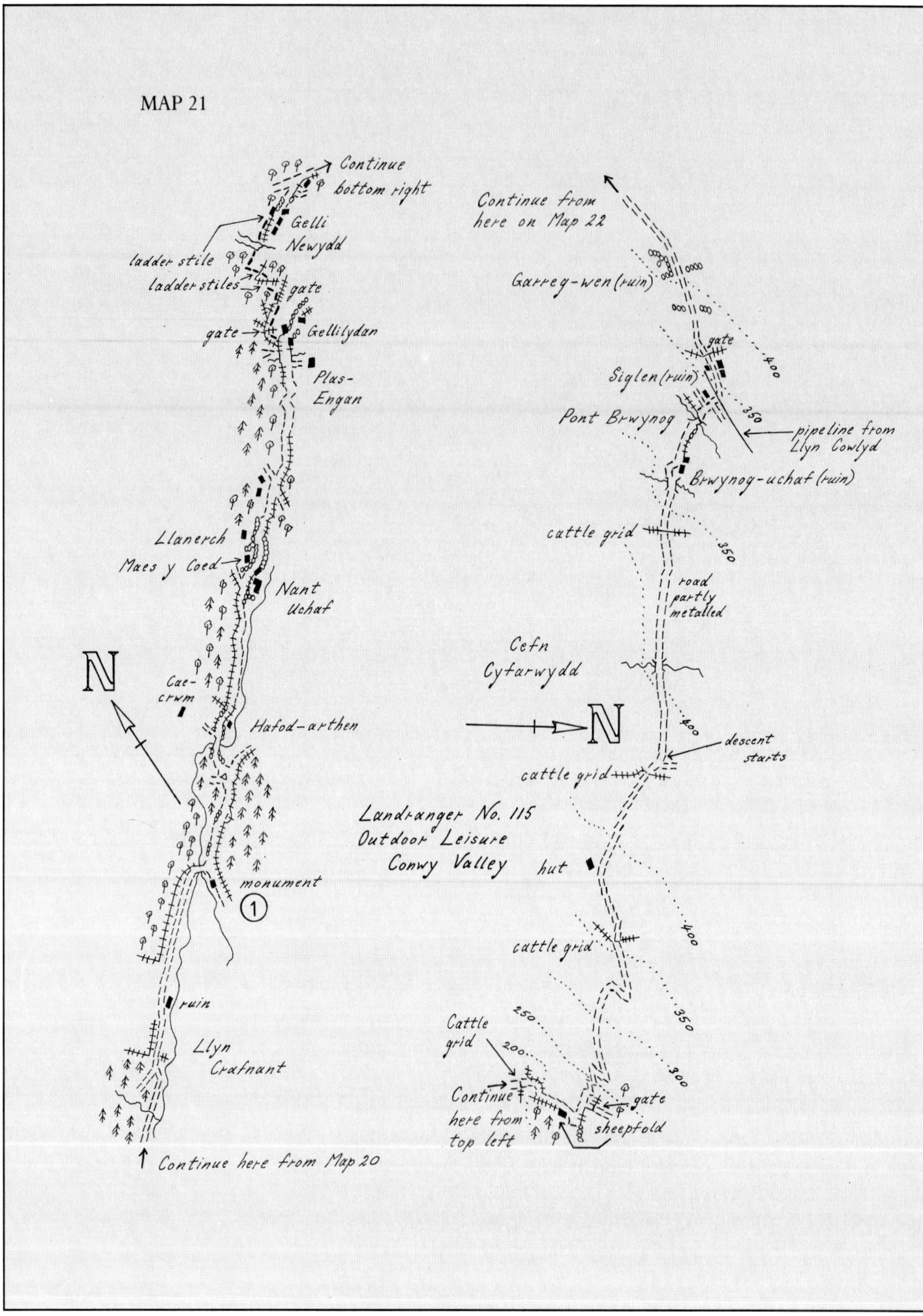
MAP 21
Continue bottom right
Gelli Newydd
ladder stile
ladder stiles
gate
gate
Gellilydan
Plas-Engan
Llanerch
Maes y Coed
Nant Uchaf
Cae-crwm
Hafod-arthen
monument
1
ruin
Llyn Crafnant
Continue here from Map 20
Landranger No. 115
Outdoor Leisure
Conwy Valley
Continue from here on Map 22
Garreg-wen (ruin)
gate
Siglen (ruin)
400
350
Pont Brwynog
pipeline from Llyn Cowlyd
Brwynog-uchaf (ruin)
cattle grid
350
road partly metalled
Cefn Cyfarwydd
400
descent starts
cattle grid
hut
400
cattle grid
350
250
Cattle grid
200
300
Continue here from top left
gate
sheepfold

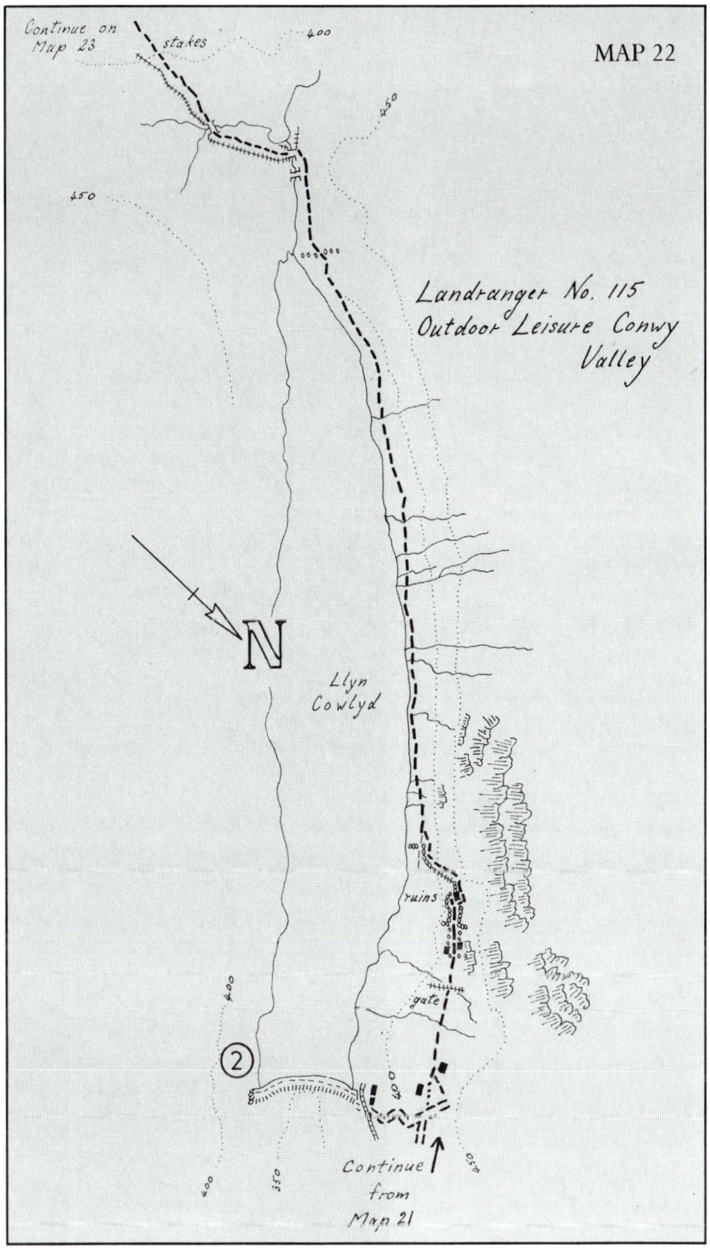

Plas-Engan, on your R, immediately afterwards crossing a small bridge. Go through the second gate on the L after the bridge, just before the road swings to the R around a cottage, Gellilydan. Follow the path into the wood, soon bending R to a second gate. Continue ahead to a third gate where the fence goes to the R of the path. After 45 yards (40 m) at a 'Walking Man' sign turn L, bending R after a few yards to a ladder stile. Turn L to climb to a further ladder stile; beyond continue by a

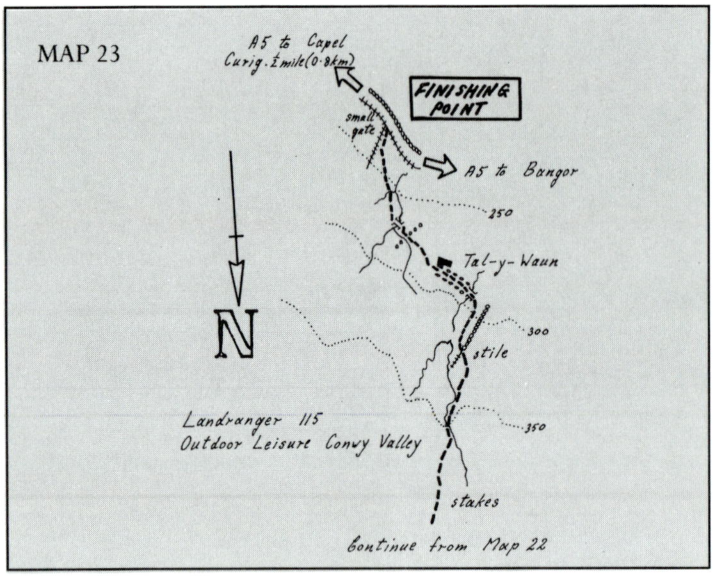

stream. After 100 yards (90 m) turn R leaving the wood after about 75 yards (70 m); there are yellow waymarks throughout this section. Cross the field beyond and then a stream. Keep by a fence to a ladder stile by a farm (Gelli Newydd). Turn L up the farm road to a junction. Turn L.

Follow this lovely old road (unfenced and only partly metalled) for 2¼ miles (3.6 km) as it slowly climbs and then descends the long ridge of Cefn Cyfarwydd (ignore a road going R after 500 yards [450 m]). In the valley cross a small bridge and up the farm road ahead going under a large pipe. Keep along this farm road past the abandoned farms of Siglen and Garreg-wen. After ½ mile (800 m) from the pipe reach a junction. The dam of Llyn Cowlyd is down to the L *(2)*.

Keep ahead across the moor to pass to the R of a small ruin after 60 yards (55 m). Here pick up a path which leads in the same direction to the L of a further ruin and on to a ladder stile in a fence. Keep ahead towards a ruined farmhouse. Reach the farmhouse by a footpath between walls. Go round to the R of the farmhouse and walk on with a wall and fence on the L, dropping diagonally down towards the lake to reach a lower path running parallel with the shore. Turn R and continue along this path with the lake on the L. The path is rough at first but gradually improves. At the end of the lake, climb with a stream to the L, then crossing it over the second of two bridges.

Continue along a path with a fence on the L to a bridge. Cross and continue in the same direction with the fence still on the L. Soon leave the fence and go downhill (there are stakes at

Track south of Llyn Cowlyd Reservoir

intervals). Eventually cross a stile and a marshy area and continue descending, bending R with the wall to the R. Lower down, turn L over a stream and go between broken walls to a farm (Tal-y-Waun). Pass the farm and continue down by some telegraph poles to reach the main Bangor–Capel Curig road (A5). Turn L along the road back to Capel Curig.

1 *Monument at Llyn Crafnant*
The obelisk set on four stone steps at the outflow of Llyn Crafnant 'Was erected by the inhabitants of Llanrwst to commemorate the gift to that town, of this lake with 19 acres of land and Cynllwyd cottage by Richard James Esqre., Dyffryn Aur, Llanrwst. AD 1896'.

2 *Llyn Cowlyd Reservoir*
Llyn Cowlyd was originally a natural lake that was first dammed about 1900 by the Conwy and Colwyn Bay Water Board to supply water to that area. In 1922 a second and higher dam was built, about 200 yards (183 m) away to increase the capacity still further. Water is taken from the lake at the dam by a steel pipeline to the Dolgarrog power station on the Afon Conwy. The waterfalls at the south-west corner of the lake are fed from a leat bringing water from high ground to the east and further water comes into the lake by tunnel from Llyn Eigiau. Llyn Cowlyd is the deepest lake in the Park, being 230 ft (70 m) deep.

The dam had a narrow escape on New Year's Eve of 1924 when water overflowed the top, washing away a considerable portion of the downstream embankment. Fortunately the concrete core held, thus averting a major disaster.

Llyn Crafnant from Coed Maes-mawr

2·17

The Central Rhinogydd

STARTING AND FINISHING POINT
Maes-y-garnedd, Cwm Nantcol (124-642269). From the A496 road from Barmouth to Harlech, turn R at Llanbedr (Sign to Cwm Nantcol). After 1 mile (1.6 km) turn R over a bridge and then immediately L. Continue along narrow road to its end at Maes-y-garnedd.
LENGTH
$6\frac{1}{2}$ miles (10.5 km)
ASCENT
2600 ft (790 m)

The ascent of Rhinog Fach from Bwlch Drws Ardudwy (The Pass of the Door of Ardudwy) is hard, much of it over steep slopes covered with boulders half-concealed by bracken and heather — typical Rhinog walking. The ridge beyond, which links Rhinog Fach to Y Llethr by the dark and sinister waters of Llyn Hywel is, however, a walk of some considerable quality. Some scrambling is necessary to reach the top of Y Llethr, but beyond that no further difficulties should be found on the long descent back into Cwm Nantcol.

Route Description (Map 24)

Start at the gate of the farm of Maes-y-garnedd *(1)* by a PFS. Take the path away from the road, crossing a small stream and a gate. The clear path is well-marked, first by white posts and then by cairns. Follow it keeping near and to the L of a stone wall that leads into the deep pass of Bwlch Drws Ardudwy between the impressive peaks of Rhinog Fawr (L) and Rhinog Fach (R). Eventually pass through a gate to enter the Rhinog National Nature Reserve *(2)*; shortly afterwards where the wall bends R, turn with it to leave the path and go to a stream. Cross a wall there at a low point (it is a ruined wall) and then the stream beyond using a small grassy island.

From the stream turn half R and follow a faint path across an area of flat ground as it skirts around some rocks to reach the bottom of a stream cascading down from the hillside. Strike directly up the hillside ahead keeping to the L of — but at an angle away from — the stream (about 125° magnetic). The climb is strenuous, over boulders half concealed by heather and bracken. The great ridge of Rhinog Fach will be seen on the L with a shallow valley in front. When level with the L-hand end of the ridge, head across the mountainside (i.e. at about 70° magnetic) towards the L of the Rhinog ridge to meet a faint track, which leads up to the R into the shallow valley. Cross the

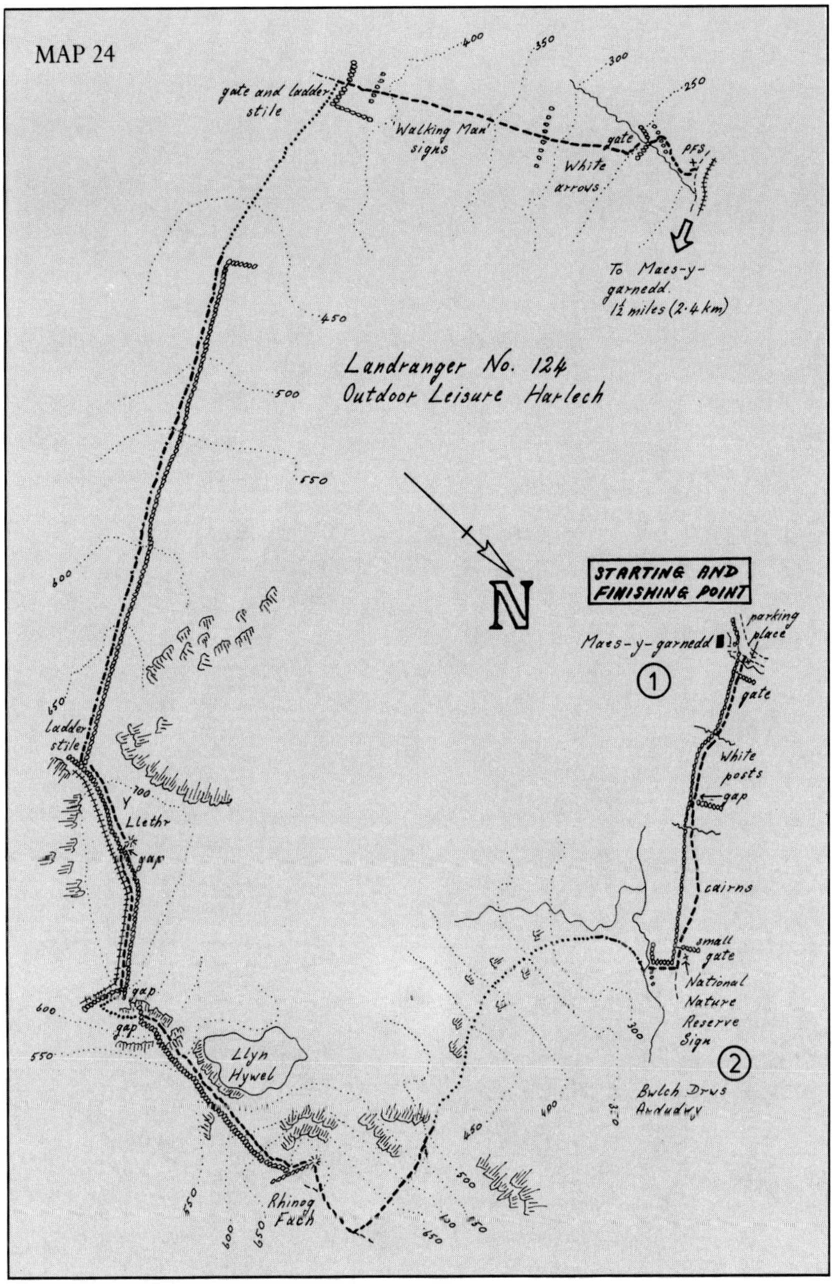

valley and a small stream and follow the path on the opposite side which leads up the side of Rhinog Fach on the L edge of an area of scree. Above the scree the path continues to rise over grassy slopes to the crest of the ridge. Turn R along the ridge to reach the summit cairn of Rhinog Fach at the end of a wall.

Do not continue along the ridge beyond the wall and cairn (there is a cliff just ahead), but instead turn L and descend to the R of the wall. Follow the wall, which soon bends to the R, down

Rhinog Fawr from road to Maes-y-garnedd

steep slopes to a col above Llyn Hywel. Follow the wall across the col and up the steep slopes ahead climbing over boulders. Where the wall ends at a rock face, cross the wall and continue in the same direction close to the rock face on the R. At the end of the rocks, go ahead to a wall and then turn R climbing up grassy slopes to a wall corner at the top. Turn L through a gap and walk along the top of the ridge between a fence (to the L) and wall (to the R). At the end, cross the wall through a gap to the R to the modest summit cairn of Y Llethr.

Return to the wall and continue in the same direction as before, descending to the right of the wall to a ladder stile. Cross and turn R. Follow a sturdy and very straight wall steadily descending for 1¼ miles (2 km) until it bends to the R on a col to form a corner. Walk across the col to a similar wall corner on the opposite side and continue as before with the wall on your R. After a few yards cross a ladder stile by a gate and follow the clear path beyond going away at a right angle to the wall. (There are 'Walking Man' signs and later white arrows.) Go down the hillside to a road. Turn R and follow the road for 1½ miles (2.4 km) back to Maes-y-garnedd.

1 *Maes-y-garnedd*
This farm was the birthplace of John Jones, one of the signatories of the death warrant of Charles I after the Civil War and husband of Cromwell's sister Catherine. He went to London as an apprentice and at the start of the Civil War in 1642 joined the Parliamentary Forces. He rose rapidly in rank, becoming a Captain of Infantry and later a Colonel and Member of Parliament and eventually Commissioner of Parliament for the Government of Ireland. After the Restoration he was put to death along with other regicides.

2 *Rhinog National Nature Reserve* See page 48.

Looking east from Rhinog Fach

2·18

The Ascent of Cnicht

STARTING AND FINISHING POINT
Beddgelert (115-591481)
LENGTH
$11\frac{1}{2}$ miles (19 km)
ASCENT
1925 ft (590 m)

From the road between Beddgelert and Tremadog, the pointed peak of Cnicht bears some resemblance to the Matterhorn, and for this reason it has been called the Welsh Matterhorn, but in reality the peak is merely the end of a long ridge and from other directions this resemblance vanishes. Neither, of course, is there any similarity whatsoever in difficulty, for the only strenuous section on Cnicht is the final rise to the summit and that is both short and easy. But the route, nevertheless, is a fine one with a long approach, which includes the Pass of Aberglaslyn and a grand ridge beyond the summit that gives first-rate views. The return to Beddgelert is an excellent walk by Llyn yr Adar (The Lake of the Birds) and Llyn Llagi into Nant Gwynant.

Route Description (Maps 8, 25–27)—see also page 50

From the bridge in Beddgelert, turn down the narrow side road with the river on the L. Just before the footbridge at the end, turn R through a small gate (sign 'To Gelert's Grave'). Pass the side path which leads to Gelert's Grave (see Route 7, page 56) and go through two small gates keeping on the R bank of the river to a bridge, there cross to the opposite bank. Follow the clear track on the opposite side which goes in the same general direction as before. The path follows the old track of the Welsh Highland Railway (see Route 7, page 54) through two small tunnels and finally through a long tunnel. (The long tunnel can be avoided by taking a path down by the river on the R as far as Pont Aber Glaslyn [see Route 7, page 54]; there, turn L up the road to rejoin the route just before Nantmor.)

At the end of the long tunnel, continue along the track ahead over a valley to a ladder stile and beyond to a road. Turn L and follow the road *(1)* through Nantmor for $1\frac{1}{4}$ miles (2 km) to a T-junction at Bwlchgwernog. Here, continue up the farm road directly opposite. Follow this splendid farm road over moorland through three gates for 1 mile (1.6 km) to cross a stream at a bridge. Beyond the bridge, continue on the farm road as it rises to a ladder stile by a gate.

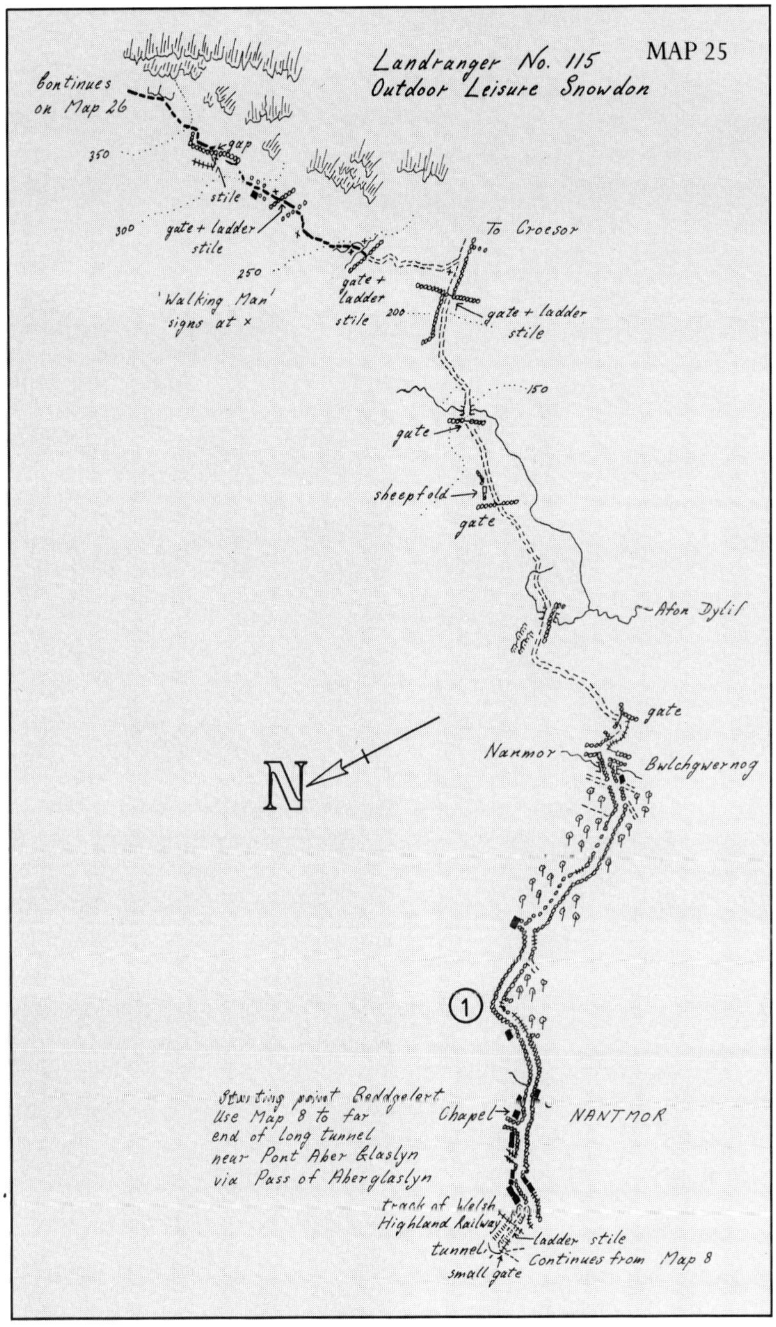

Soon after the gate take a path going back half L ('Walking Man' sign) just before the farm road starts to descend through woods towards Croesor. Follow the clear track past a ruin on the R to a ladder stile by a gate. Continue ahead to the L of a stream, soon crossing to the R bank. Leave to the R of the stream, to reach a ladder stile on the ridge (there are further 'Walking Man' signs on this section). Beyond, continue to a wall

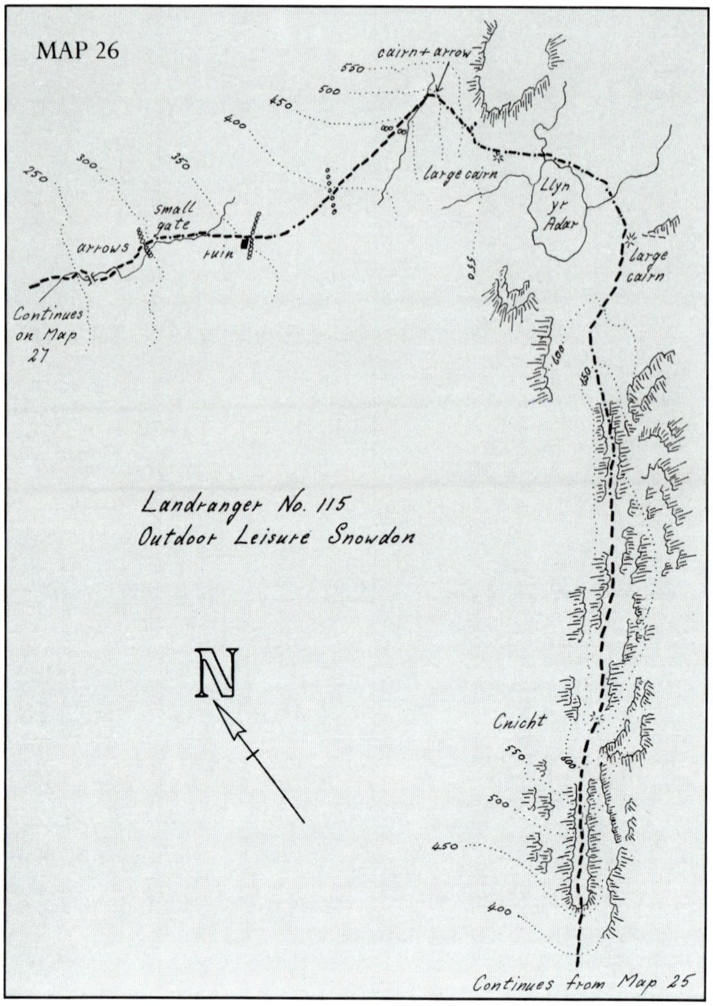

and follow this (i.e. with wall to the R) to a stile and gap, there cross and continue now with the wall on the L. At the end, follow the wall up scree to the R, round the top of the wall and up to the ridge. Follow the ridge up steeply to the summit of Cnicht.

Continue beyond the summit along the ridge following a path which gradually descends further along. Eventually, reach a large cairn with a lake, Llyn yr Adar, to the L. Turn L and follow a faint path down to the lake. Keep the lake on the L to cross a small stream and continue in the same direction gradually leaving the lake on a faint path (there are a few cairns) to reach a large cairn. Here the path descends steeply, bending L lower down (cairn and arrows). The path goes to the R of a stream for

The hills south of Llyn Dinas

Cnicht from Beddgelert-Tremadog road

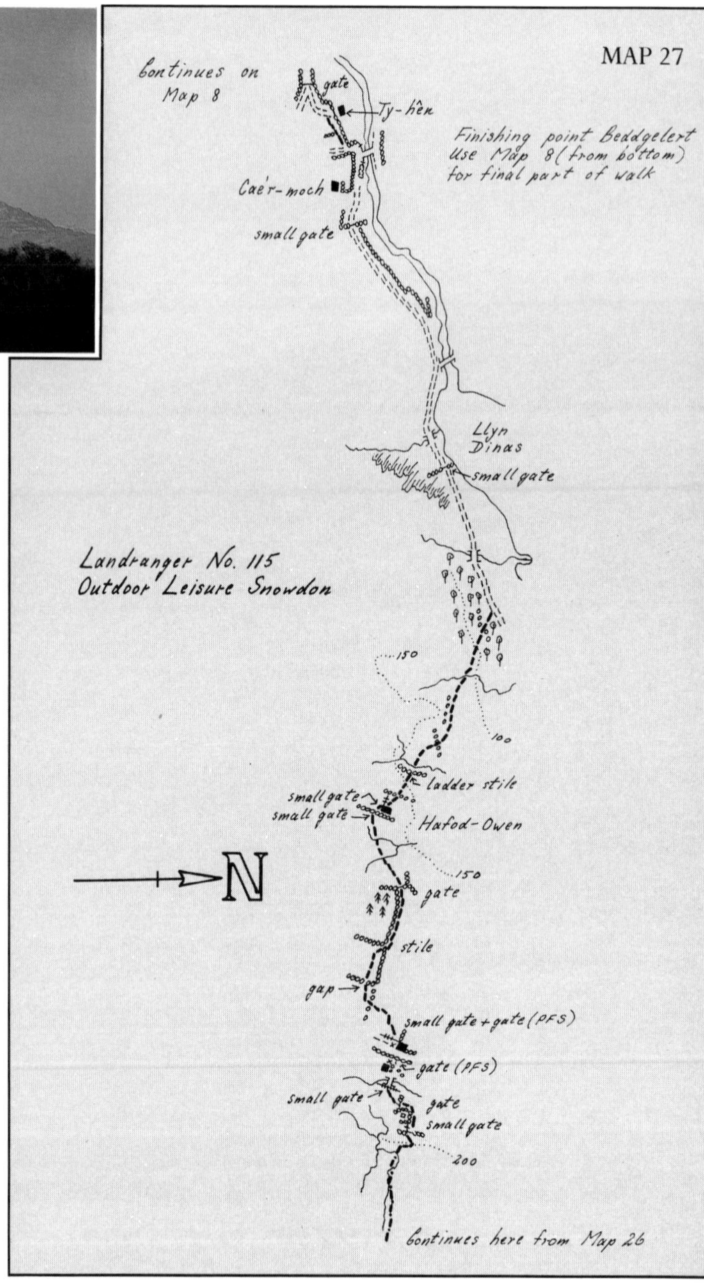

a short distance, then becomes clearer as it leaves the stream to the R through a wall gap. Beyond, continue to descend on a very good path to a further wall gap. The path becomes more indistinct beyond this gap, but goes to still another gap by a small ruined barn. Below the barn the path follows near to a stream and becomes indefinite, crossing marshy ground to reach a small gate.

Continue with the path as it crosses the stream to the L bank and then back to the R bank. (There are some cairns and painted arrows on this section which will help — generally, keep near to the stream and head towards a white house on the road.) Eventually, drop down by rocks and pass through a few trees to reach a gate in a wall. From the gate, descend with a fence and then a wall on the L to pass and then bend to the L behind a cottage. At the rear of the cottage go through a gate and down half R to a further gate; there rise to the R of a second cottage to reach a road opposite a white house.

Go through a small gate to the L of the house (PFS) and follow a path half L up a small hill. Cross a wall gap, bend R to a second gap, and then descend with a wall on your R. At the end go over a stile and continue, this time with a wall on the L, to a gate by some conifers. From this point the path leaves the wall and goes half L to descend and then ascend to a small cottage, Hafod Owen. At the cottage, go through a white gate and round L of the building to a second gate. At the rear of the cottage, go through a gap in some bushes and over a wall. The path is now clear, slowly dropping down the hillside to a ladder stile; beyond, it continues across the hillside crossing two ravines to eventually enter a wood. Drop down through the wood to a farm road by a lake and turn L. The prominent hill on the opposite side of the valley to your R after turning is Dinas Emrys (see Route 7 page 52).

Follow the farm road by the lake (Llyn Dinas) to eventually reach a bridge. Do not cross, but continue on the L bank of the stream passing a cottage (Cae'r-moch) and a tunnel of rhododendron bushes to a second bridge. Again, do not cross, but turn L up a lane passing through a gap. Immediately after the gap, turn R, and follow a path to the L of a wall to reach the end of a lane at a gate. Follow the lane for nearly $\frac{3}{4}$ mile (1.2 km) to a bridge. Go through a small gate on the L just before the bridge and follow the river on its L bank to the footbridge in Beddgelert. Cross and go into the village.

1 Carneddi (The Place of Stones)

The farm of Carneddi lies on the rising slopes of Moel y Dyniewyd on the opposite side of Dolfriog Wood from the river Nanmor. In 1945 the farm was bought by new owners, a family from an English city whose experience of farming was confined to the keeping of a few household pets. Their life at Carneddi has been wonderfully told in two books which can be found on sale in most local bookshops. *Place of Stones* takes their story up to 1960 and *Hill Farm Story* to 1966. Both were written by Ruth Janette Ruck, one of the two daughters of the family.

2·19

The Traverse of Snowdon

STARTING POINT
Bethania (115-627506) on the A498 3 miles (5 km) from Beddgelert.
FINISHING POINT
Pen-y-Pass (115-647557)
LENGTH
10 miles (16 km)
ASCENT
2400 ft (730 m)

The Horseshoe is by far the most difficult of the usual routes up Snowdon, but the Miners' Track and the Watkin Path have the greatest interest. This route uses the Watkin Path for the ascent and the Miners' Track for the descent. Both paths are well-marked throughout and for most of their length give no difficulty in walking. The difficult sections are the final rise of the Watkin Path over steep scree to the summit of Yr Wyddfa, and the descent down the Miners' Track as far as Glaslyn.

Route Description (Maps 28–30)

Leave the car-park at Bethania into the main road and turn L. Walk along the road, soon turning R down a small lane over a cattle grid (sign 'Public Footpath to Snowdon'). This is the start of the Watkin Path *(1)*. Continue up the lane soon leaving the tarmac road to the L up a rough road (sign 'Llwybr Watkin Path'). Further along, pass through a gate and continue to follow the old mine road, soon with open ground on both sides. The path swings R then L, with a river below on the R. As you climb, there is a good view of waterfalls ahead and the track passes over the old tramway from the South Snowdon Slate Quarry. Beyond, go through a gate to enter the Yr Wyddfa-Snowdon National Nature Reserve *(2) (3)*.

The path continues to the L of the stream, but crosses a bridge to the R bank just before the ruin at Plas Cwm Llan *(4)*. Pass the ruin and the Gladstone Rock *(5)* further along and proceed to the miners' barracks and quarries. At the barracks, the path swings R keeping to the R of a large waste heap. The path from here is rougher and rises more steeply, but is very clear and in any case is well-marked with cairns and the occasional sign. Continue up the mountainside to reach a large cairn on a col with a path coming in from the R (this is the path from Y Lliwedd); here go L and cross the col. On the far side of the col, the path rises very steeply, slanting L up a great

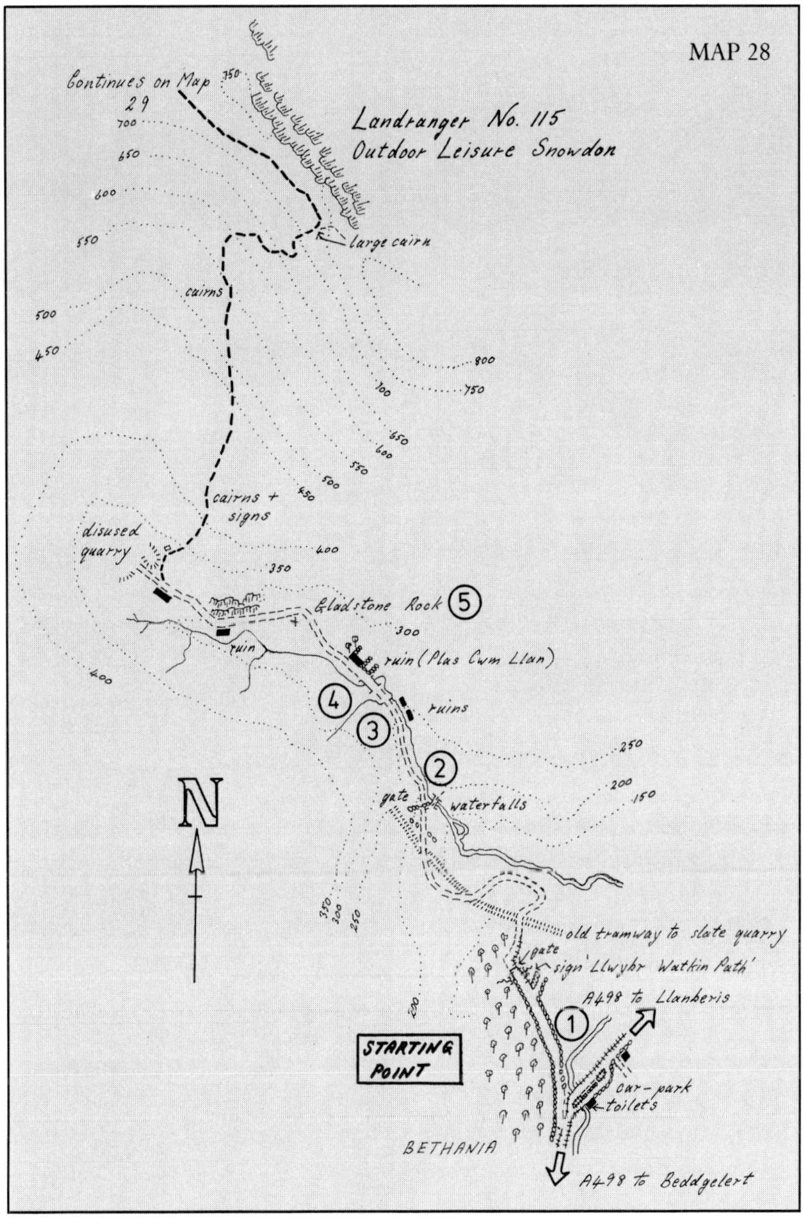

shattered face of scree and rock. Reach the ridge at the top (rock monolith) and turn R for a short distance to the Summit Hotel *(6) (7) (8)*.

Leave the Summit Hotel at the far end (i.e. from the station) and descend on the path by the railway track to reach a rock monolith on Bwlch Glas. (Note: there is a second monolith lower down where the Snowdon Ranger Path meets the railway line.) Here drop to the R from the ridge down zig-zags at the top of the Miners' Track. Descend the Miners' Track until a junction of paths is reached above a lake (Glaslyn), here

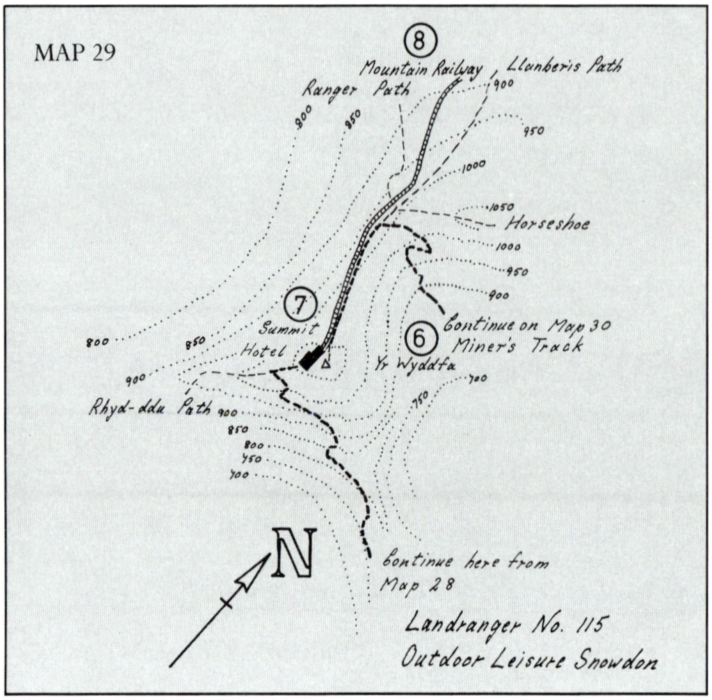

descend steeply to the R to reach the lake by the ruins of some old miners' barracks (9). (Do not go too far to the R, where there are dangerous mines.) Turn L to follow the broad path around the L shore of the lake and continue on, eventually reaching a lower and larger lake, Llyn Llydaw. Keep on the L shore of this lake past old mine buildings *(9) (10)*, later, to cross a causeway *(11)*. Follow the clear path beyond the lake *(12)* and down by a third and lower lake, Llyn Teyrn, to eventually reach Pen-y-Pass *(13)*.

1 The Watkin Path

This path was constructed by Sir Edward Watkin who, in the late eighteenth century, acquired an area of land near Bethania in the valley of Nant Gwynant; his house, called The Chalet, was built in the woods there. The path was intended to connect his house with the summit of Snowdon and was opened by the then Prime Minister, W. E. Gladstone, in 1892 (see below). Sir Edward, a rich and influential railway owner, should also be remembered for his attempt to construct a tunnel under the English Channel, 1 mile (1.6 km) being dug on each side before he was stopped by the Government of the day.

Y Lliwedd from Yr Wyddfa

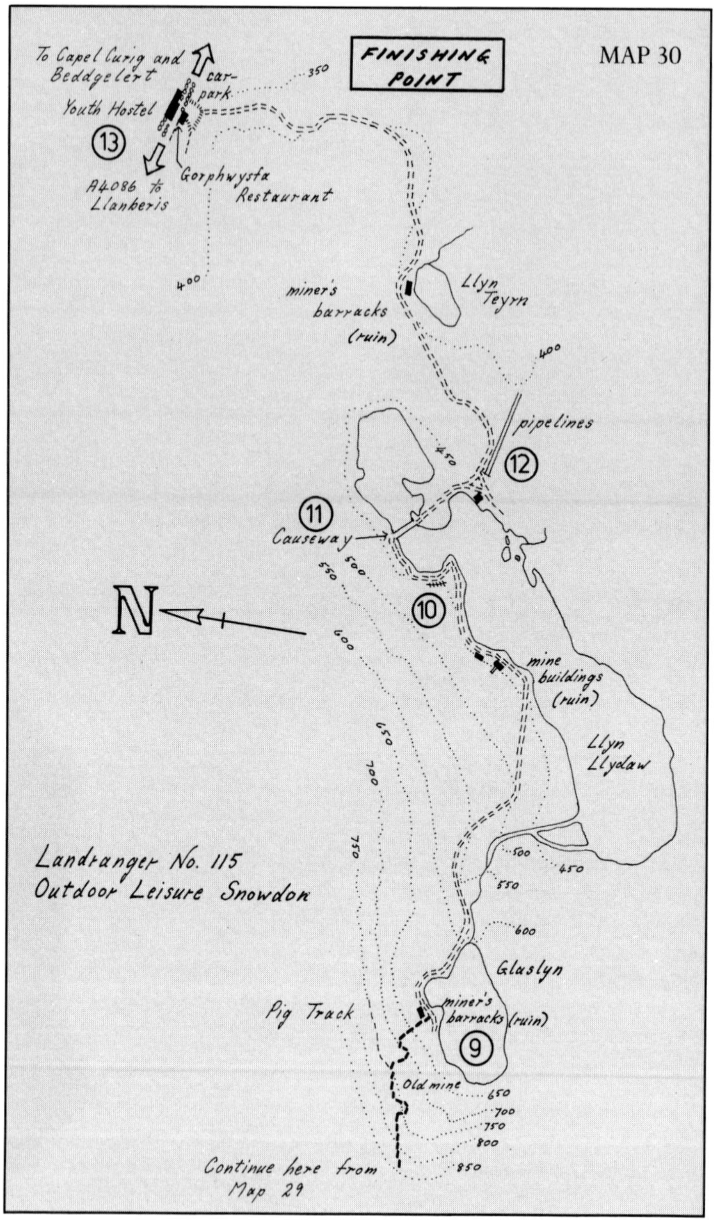

2 *Yr Wyddfa-Snowdon National Nature Reserve*
4145 acres (1678 hectares) of Snowdon were established as a National Nature Reserve by the Nature Conservancy Council (see page 16) in 1966, because of its immense interest both for its geology and for its natural history. Access is allowed throughout the area, but care should be taken not to damage any rocks, plants, boundary or enclosure fences, etc., within the area.

The Miners' Track and *Cwm y Llan*, Nature Conservancy Council.

The Youth Hostel at Pen-y-Pass

3 Erosion — the Snowdon Management Scheme

It was estimated that in 1975, a typical year, no less than 350,000 people visited the summit of Snowdon, of whom probably about two-thirds were walkers using the established footpaths. It is scarcely surprising therefore, that this resulted in a serious erosion problem on Snowdon, even though a large amount of work had already been put in to deal with it. It was also a problem that was going to become worse in the future, rather than better, as walking increased in popularity.

It was against this background that the Snowdonia National Park Authority and the Countryside Commission agreed in October 1977 on a five-year programme of work to improve the state of the footpaths and the general environment of Snowdon, and to increase facilities for visitors to the mountain. This initial programme has now been completed, but work still continues both on new projects and on regular maintenance, as it would make little sense to restore paths only to let them deteriorate again.

The main aim of this work is to protect the mountain from the people rather than the people from the mountain. Inevitably, because of the severe weather conditions prevailing for much of the year, a great deal of the work is carried out in the summer months when most holidaymakers are also there. The work, therefore, is a feature of Snowdon that visitors are very likely to see.

The methods for restoring paths have been worked out and well-tried over the years. Slabs of slate dug in vertically across a path and steps constructed from large rocks considerably reduce the surface slippage of material. Once slippage has been prevented, the surface can then be restored with smaller stones or gravel. Ditches dug alongside the path help to remove surface water, while short stretches of fence placed at strategic points discourage visitors from cutting corners or widening paths.

4 *Hafod y Llan Quarry (South Snowdon Slate Quarry)*
The Watkin Path passes close to the buildings and workings of the South Snowdon Slate Quarry, which was active from 1840 to about 1880. The dressed slate was carried by tramway down to Bethania at Nant Gwynant and from there to Porthmadog, by cart. The poor quality of the slate, the high proportion of waste and the high cost of transport were all factors that contributed to the short life of the quarry. The cutting for the tramway, the quarrymen's barracks, workshops, the manager's house (Plas Cwm Llan), spoil heaps and the quarries can all be seen from the path. The bullet holes on the far wall of the manager's house as you reach it were made by soldiers who trained in this area during World War II.

5 *The Gladstone Rock*
The granite tablet cemented into place on the low rock records, in Welsh and English:

'Sep. 13th 1892 — Upon this rock the Right Honourable W. E. Gladstone, M.P. when Prime Minister for the fourth time and 83 years old addressed the people of Eryri upon justice to Wales. The multitude sang Cymric hymns and 'The Land of My Fathers'. Publicly dedicated by Sir Edward and Lady Watkin June 1893'.

The occasion was the opening of the Watkin Path to the summit of Snowdon.

6 *Yr Wyddfa*
The highest point of the Snowdon massif is Yr Wyddfa, at 3559 ft (1085 m) the highest in England and Wales. It is said to be the grave of Rhita Gawr (or Fawr), a Welsh giant slain by King Arthur; hence the English meaning of its name, 'burial place'.

7 *The Summit Hotel* See page 166.

8 *The Snowdon Mountain Railway* See page 164.

9 *The Brittania Copper Mine*
The Brittania Copper Mine was working from about 1810 and probably earlier, to 1926. The actual mine is to the right as you descend to Glaslyn down the Miners' Track; the buildings on the shore of Glaslyn were miners' barracks as were those on the shore of Llyn Teyrn; the crushing plant was in the large building on the shore of Llyn Llydaw; both

A distant view of the Snowdon Horseshoe

the Miners' Track and the causeway were constructed to enable ore to be carried down to the valley at Pen-y-Pass (see page 148).

10 *Moraines and Ice-smoothed Rock in Cwm Dyli*

Signs of the Ice Age in North Wales are very obvious in the cymoedd of Snowdon. At several points along the Miners' Track you will see rock smoothed by the moving ice, and just before the causeway the path skirts around some low hills (moraines) made up from the rock debris of the glacier. The isolated rocks lying about the slopes were once carried on the ice but left behind as the ice retreated for the last time.

11 *The Causeway*

The north-east reach of Llyn Llydaw is cut by a causeway which carried the Miners' Track to the northern shore. The history of the causeway is described on a slate slab fixed to a rock wall nearby:

'The Llydaw Causeway. This causeway was built by the Cwmdyle Rock and Green Lake Copper Mining Company under the direction of the mine captain, Thomas Colliver. During its construction the level of the lake was lowered 12 ft and 6000 cubic yards of waste rock from the mine were used to build the embankment. The causeway was first crossed on 13 October, 1853.'

The causeway was restored to its former height by the Park Authority.

12 *The Hydro-electric Power Station of Cwm Dyli*

Two steel pipelines, 30 in (76 cm) in diameter, run from the eastern end of Llyn Llydaw through Cwm Dyli for about $1\frac{1}{4}$ miles (2 km) to a power station situated at the head of Nant Gwynant. The water from Llyn Llydaw, falling through 1100 ft (335 m), builds up a pressure of nearly 500 lb/sq in (3.45 Megapascals) at the bottom end of the pipeline and is used to drive three turbines which supply electricity both locally and to the National Grid.

The power station was built in 1906 from local stone and blends well with its surroundings. Its output of 5 Megawatts is small in comparison with some other power stations in North Wales, but hydro-electricity is cheap and does not involve the burning of valuable irreplaceable fuels. It can also be operational in a very short time, about twenty-five minutes, to meet any sudden increase in demand.

13 *Pen-y-Pass* See page 163.

3·20

The Nantlle Ridge

STARTING POINT
Rhyd-ddu (115-571526), $3\frac{1}{2}$ miles (5.5 km) from Beddgelert along the Caernarfon road (A4085)
FINISHING POINT
Nebo (115-479505), about 1 mile (1.6 km) east of the Porthmadog-Caernarfon road (A487)
LENGTH
$7\frac{1}{2}$ miles (12 km)
ASCENT
2988 ft (910 m)

This is one of the finest ridge walks in North Wales, ranking with the Snowdon Horseshoe and the ridge of the Carneddau. Its eastern end is well-frequented but the western summits, being more isolated, are usually lonely. There are a few stretches of scrambling, but these can usually be avoided by taking easier lines nearby. The views from the ridge, into Cwm Pennant on the left and the Nantlle valley on the right, are remarkable.

Route Description (Maps 31–33)

Walk from the car-park at Rhyd-ddu *(1)* into the road (A4085) and cross to a small gate on the opposite side (PFS). Take the R-hand path towards a farm which soon reaches a bridge. Do not cross, but turn L along the river bank to a second bridge. Cross this bridge; after a stile go half R to a farm road and follow this to the R to reach a gate leading into a road (PFS). Do not go through the gate, but instead turn L through a small gate and follow a path with a wall on the R. At a fence (after bends on the wall) go through a gap and turn L with the fence on the L. Where the fence bends away L, continue up the mountainside to a ladder stile and then to a large boulder marked with white arrows. Take the R-hand path (sign 'Ridge') steeply uphill (faint white arrows) to a further ladder stile. The path continues up to reach still another ladder stile in a wall on the ridge top. Cross to the summit cairn of Y Garn.

Return to the ladder stile and, after crossing, turn R to follow the ridge with the wall to the R. Later, cross the wall to follow a path near to the edge. (The route along the edge has some exciting moments with magnificent views down the considerable cliff to the R. An alternative route may be followed, however, just down from the crest to the L, which cuts out both the exciting moments and the views.) Reach the top of Mynydd Drws-y-coed and cross a ladder stile in a fence. Continue along the ridge to the summit of Trum y Ddysgl and then descend approximately south-west down a grassy ridge. After about 300 yards (275 m) branch R approximately due east to descend a

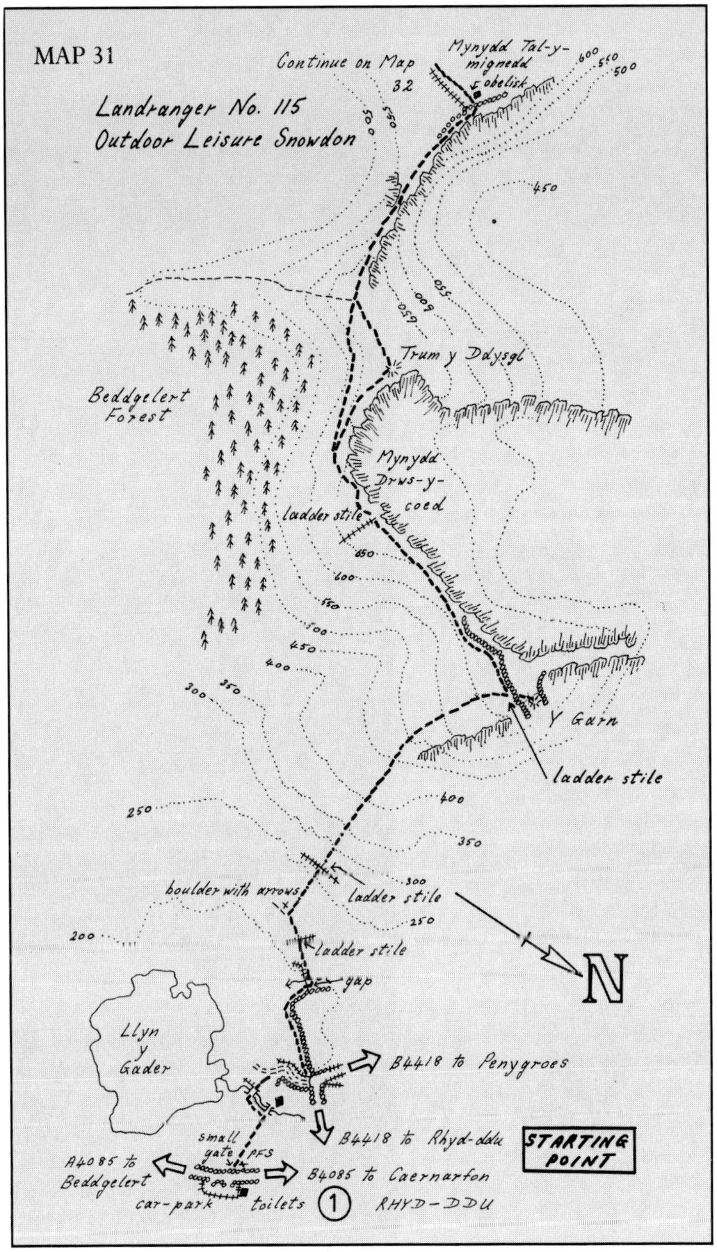

narrow grass ridge which gradually becomes still narrower, until a collapsed section is reached. Cross and climb the ridge beyond to the large obelisk on Mynydd Tal-y-mignedd.

From the obelisk continue down a ridge to the L (i.e. SW) with a fence to the L. Follow the clear path by the fence eventually to descend steeply into the col of Bwlch Dros-bern (crossing and re-crossing the fence at ladder stiles). At the far side of the col where the wall (i.e. at the end of the fence) reaches a rock face, scramble up the rocks at a convenient point

Opposite *Looking back from the lower slopes of Y Garn over Llyn y Gader*

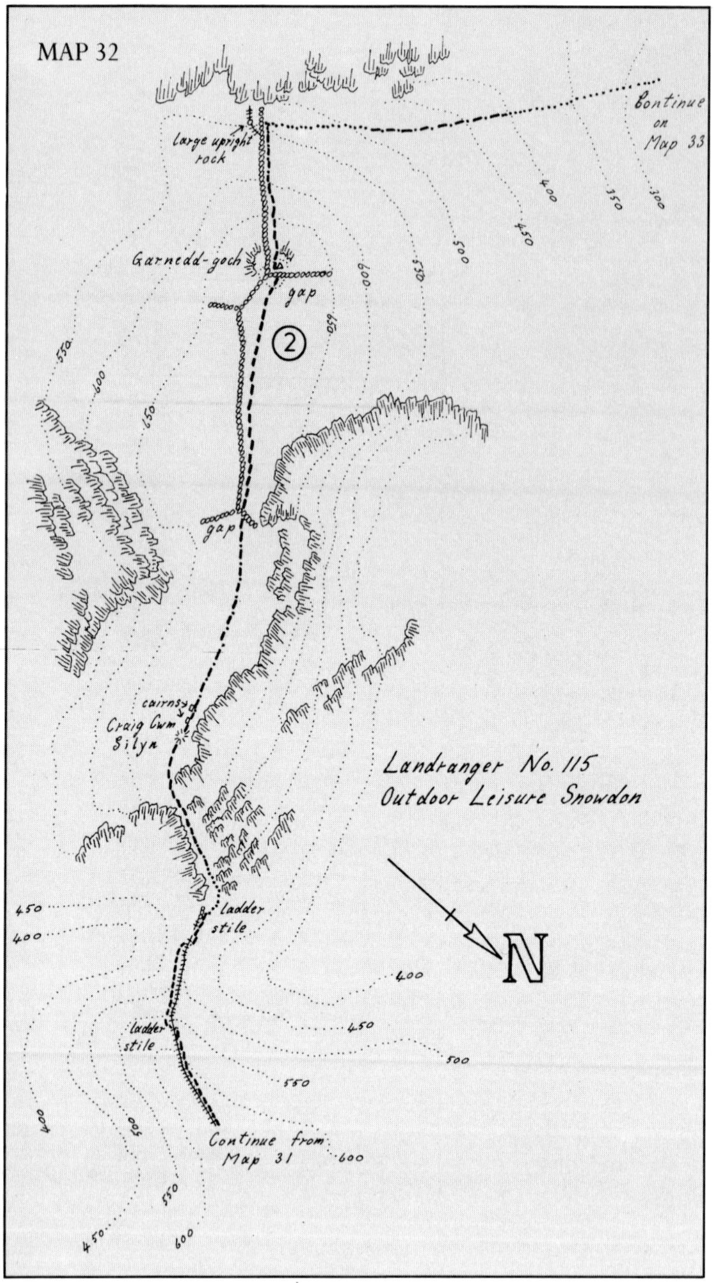

to pick up a path at the top. Continue up the ridge beyond, to reach the large summit cairn of Craig Cwm Silyn, and then along the top of the ridge, past two prominent cairns, to a wall. Go through a gap and then on in the same direction with the wall to the L to reach a gap in a further wall. The OS obelisk of Garnedd-goch *(2)* is just over the wall on the opposite side.

View SSW from Y Garn on the Nantlle Ridge

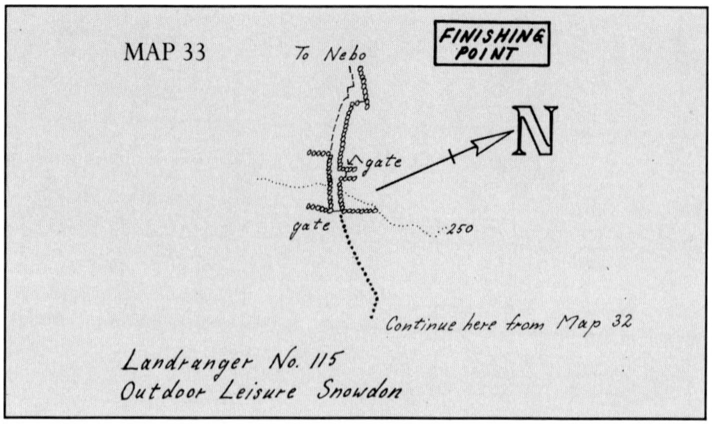

Beyond the obelisk continue in the same direction now descending with the wall still on the L; where the hillside steepens (a fence begins by a tall rock on the opposite side of the wall) turn R to contour the hillside. The path is faint at first but improves later and is waymarked by short upright stones. Descend to a large moorland area to the R of a lake and cross to an obvious walled lane on the opposite side. Enter the lane by a gate and follow it to its end where it bends R to a road. Follow the road to Nebo.

1 *Welsh Highland Railway* (See page 54.)
The railway followed the A4085 closely on its eastern side from near Pitt's Head to Rhyd-ddu, north of which it went further to the east along a winding track past Llyn Cwellyn. There were stations by the present Snowdon Ranger Youth Hostel and at the car-park at Rhyd-ddu.

2 *Slate Quarries in the Nantlle Valley*
The Nantlle Valley was the scene of some of the biggest slate quarries in North Wales, although not on the scale of those at Llanberis and Bethesda. The slate was extracted from open pits in the valley floor. The biggest were the Dorothea, which worked from about 1829, the Penyrorsedd from about 1816 and the Talysarn. The quarries can be easily seen from the crest of the Nantlle Ridge about the summit of Garnedd-goch.

3·21

The Southern Rhinogydd

STARTING AND FINISHING POINT
Tal-y-bont (124-590218) on the A496 road from Barmouth to Harlech, 4 miles (6.5 km) from Barmouth.
LENGTH
$12\frac{1}{2}$ miles (20 km)
ASCENT
3275 ft (1000 m)

South of the summit of Y Llethr the Rhinogydd is an area of rounded grassy hills which form a horseshoe of summits from Moelfre in the west to Llawlech in the south. The long approach to the horseshoe from Tal-y-bont adds to the distance, but a fair pace can be maintained throughout as the way underfoot is not difficult and the climbing is well spread out over the miles. As might be expected, the views from the ridge are extensive throughout. The southern Rhinogydd are remote and quiet and it is unlikely that many others will be met along the way.

Route Description (Maps 34–36)

In Tal-y-bont go up the narrow lane at the northern end of the bridge (i.e. on the Harlech side) by toilets, a car-park and telephone kiosks. Continue past the Old Country Life Centre (museum) and on between a hedge and a wall to reach a stream. Keep on the clear path through woods to the L of the river, ignoring any paths coming in from the L and bridges over the stream to the R. Eventually the path rises to the L up a slope to reach a small cottage, 'Lletty-lloegr'. There, turn L up a road and R up a path which bends R behind the cottage.

At the rear of the cottage do not go through a gap in a crossing wall but turn L to follow the wall uphill. At a small watercourse with a raised bank, turn L to follow it to a wall, there crossing the stone stile nearby into a lane. Turn R and follow the lane between walls for $1\frac{1}{4}$ miles (2 km); on the way it bends sharp R and then L. Finally, where the walls end go through a gate and continue on a wide track over the open moor with a wood on the slope to the L. Pass a small path branching R and at a junction (with cairn) again keep L. Beyond the wood and screes to the L turn up the slope L to reach a wall on the ridge top. From here, there is a good view across to Rhinog Fawr and down into Cwm Nantcol.

Turn R and follow the wall down to a col. Where the wall

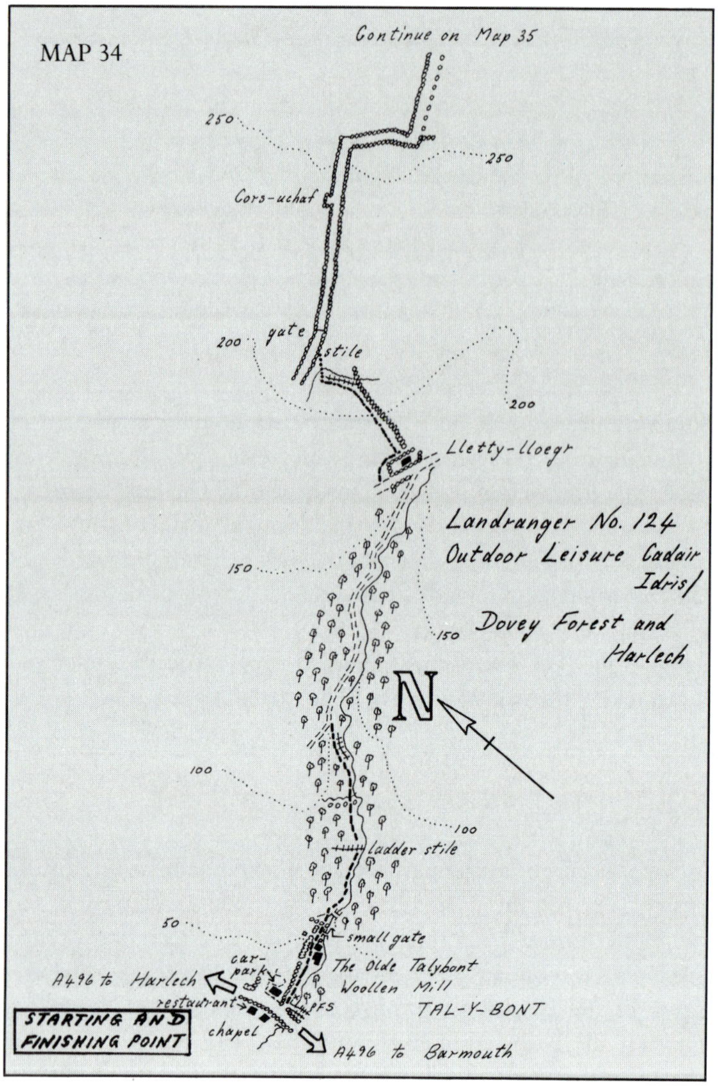

bends L to form a wall corner, cross the col in approximately the same direction to a wall corner on the opposite side. Again continue in the same direction with a wall on L rising slowly for 1 mile (1.6 km) to a wall corner, here go over a ladder stile to the L. Climb steeply up the hill to a small cairn on a flat top; this is the summit cairn of Y Llethr.

Return to the ladder stile. Cross and continue to descend with the wall on the L, i.e. to the R from your original direction. No difficulty will now be found in following the route along a spendid ridge to Diffwys *(1)* and beyond, for it is marked throughout by a sturdy wall. Eventually, descend along the ridge

Farm track around Moelyblithcwm

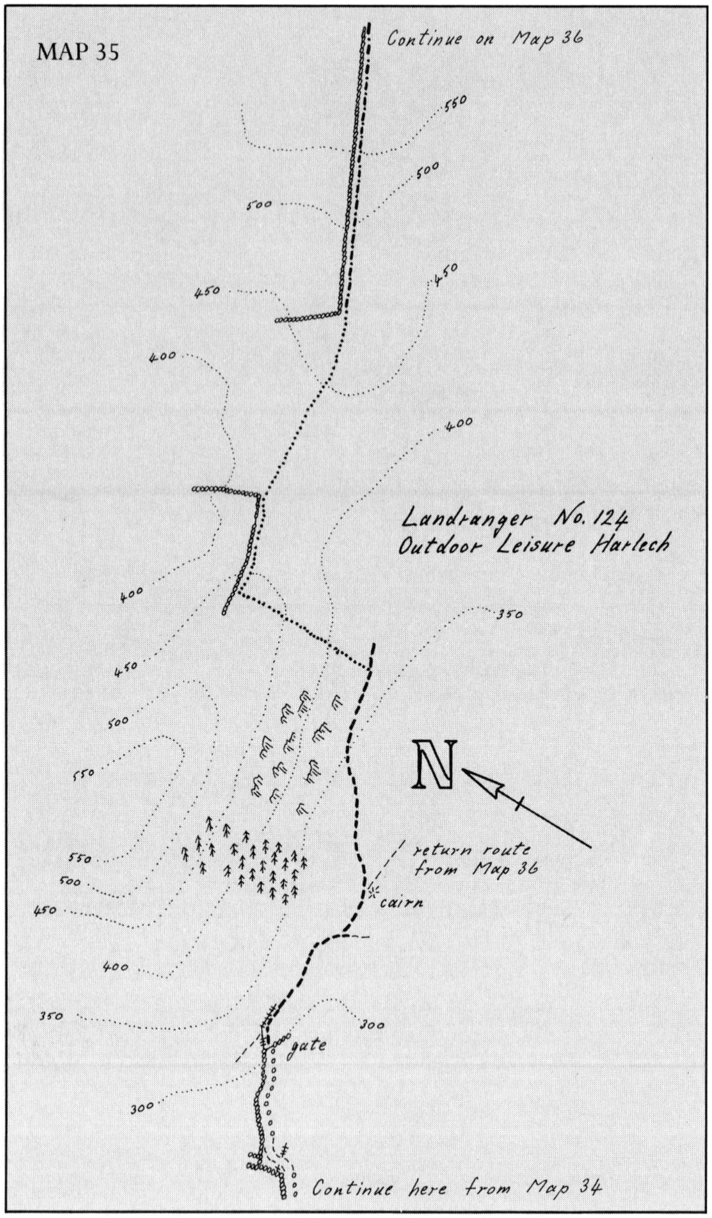

from Diffwys and then on the next rise (marked on OS maps as 642 m) at 647228 leave the ridge to the R and descend down grass slopes to the prominent bridge, Pont-Scethin, which crosses the Afon Ysgethin in the valley *(2)*. Cross the bridge and follow the track half L to rejoin the path taken earlier in the day below the wood. Turn L and retrace your steps back to Tal-y-bont.

1 The Trawsfynydd Power Station

The two square white towers seen in the distance to the right

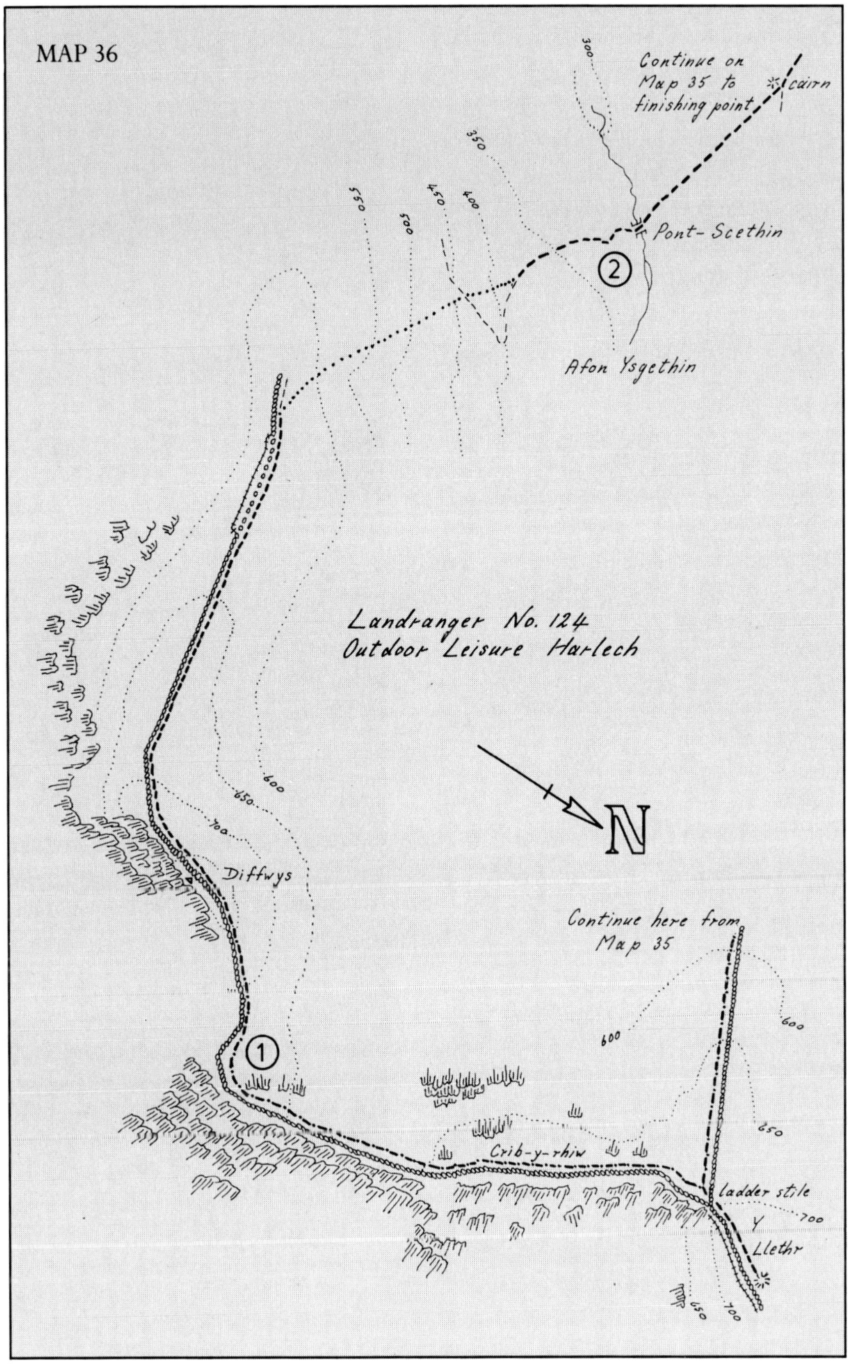

MAP 36

of Y Llethr when looking back from the start of the final climb to Diffwys are the reactor buildings of the nuclear power station at Trawsfynydd. Construction of the station began in 1959 and was completed in 1965 when it began to supply electricity into the National Grid. This was the first inland nuclear power station built by the Central Electricity Generating Board.

2 *Pont-Scethin*
This wonderful old bridge which spans the Afon Ysgethin was originally used by coaches, for it lies on the line of the old road from London to Harlech which crossed the valley here. The ruins to the right of the small wood on the slopes of Moelfre are those of an old coaching inn.

Landscape near Pont-Scethin

3·22

THE NANT FFRANCON RIDGE, Y GARN TO ELIDIR FAWR

STARTING AND FINISHING POINT
Nant Peris (115-606582), just beyond Llyn Peris on the A4086 about 2 miles (3 km) from Llanberis.
LENGTH
8½ miles (13.5 km)
ASCENT
3725 ft (1135 m)

The Nant Ffrancon Valley is bounded on its western side by a line of immense hanging valleys gouged out of the mountainside during the Ice Age, their backcloth one of the finest ridges in Wales, running in a north-westerly direction from the col of Bwlch Blaen Cwm Idwal (Pass at the head of Cwm Idwal) to the summit of Elidir Fawr. Starting from Nant Peris, a long climb is needed to reach the col, but the ridge beyond is superb with magnificent views down into the hanging valleys and into the Nant Ffrancon. From Elidir Fawr a long and steep descent first over scree and then grass is used for the return to Nant Peris.

ROUTE DESCRIPTION (Maps 37, 38)

Leave the car-park at Nant Peris *(1)* and turn R along the road *(2)*. Walk along the road for nearly ¾ mile (1.2 km). A stream, the Afon Nant-Peris, approaches the road on the R; where it comes alongside the road — and just past a bridge over it — turn L from the road up a rough path between upright slabs of slate (PFS). Pass to the R of a cottage to a gate. Keep to the L in the next field and go over a ladder stile to the L of a second cottage. Continue uphill (white arrows) with a wall over on the L to reach a stream. Here, keep on a path on the R bank of the stream to later bend R then L with a fence and wall to a ladder stile. Beyond the stile follow the wall until it turns R; turn R with it then L to reach a stream at a footbridge. Cross. The path then goes to the L of the stream before moving away to the L to a second stream. Above here the path is less distinct, but keeps generally to the R of the second stream (some cairns). Eventually near to the top cross over the stream (which ends soon afterwards in a marshy area to the R) and head on a faint track across the grassy top of a col to a lake, Llyn y Cŵn *(3)*.

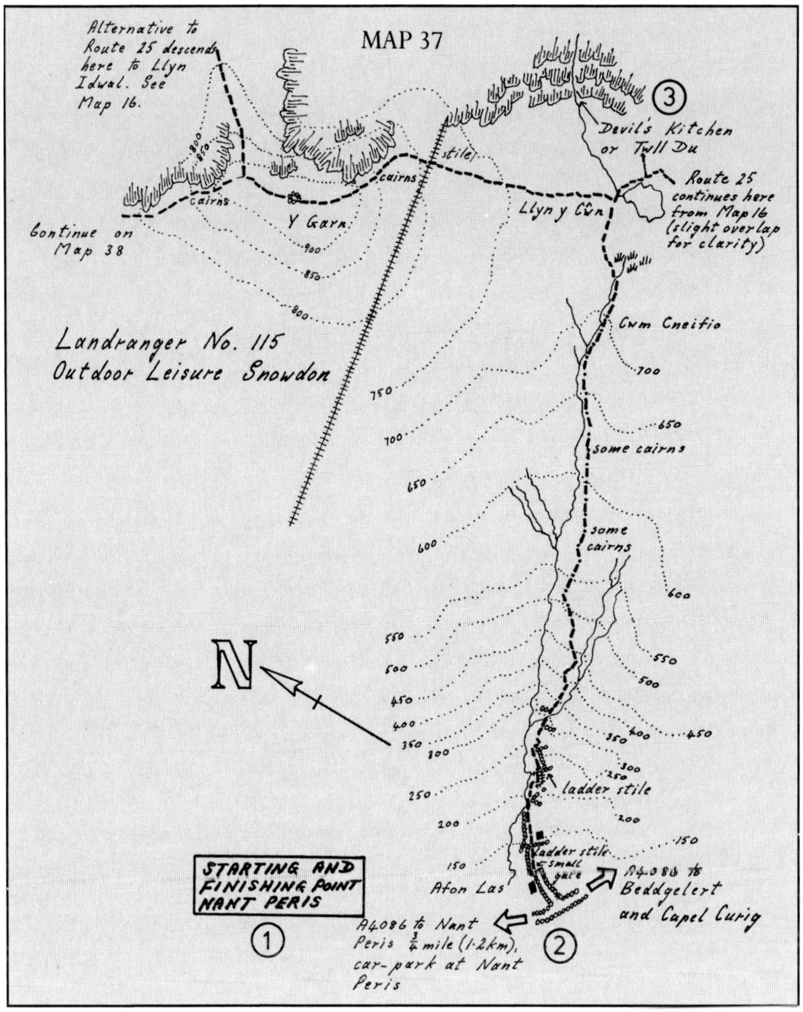

At around the mid-point of the lake turn L on a path up a grassy hill and head for Y Garn. The path up Y Garn is clear throughout and climbs steadily over grass and then scree to the summit, gradually opening up a magnificent view to the R (a fence has been erected between Llyn y Cŵn and Y Garn which should be crossed at a stile). Continue along the ridge from Y Garn to Foel-goch; the route keeps generally to the top of the ridge, passing through a series of magnificent viewpoints, of which Foel-goch is outstanding. From Foel-goch, descend steeply along a path to the L of a cliff (cairns) to reach a lower path, there turn R. (A fence has been erected to the west of Foel-goch which should be crossed at a stile.) Follow the clear path which sweeps round to the L across the hillside. As the path nears the crest on the R, just beyond a small patch of scree, go R at a path fork. The path now reaches the crest giving a superb view down into Marchlyn Mawr *(4)*. Follow the path

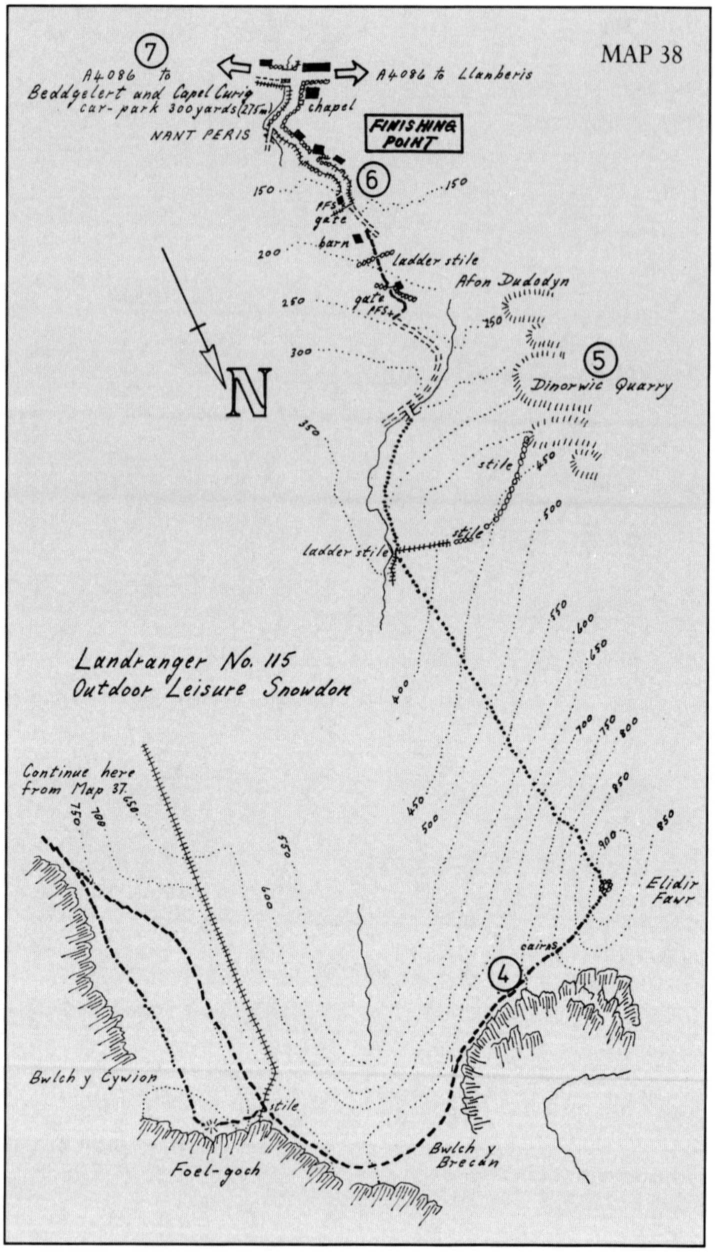

along the crest and then over grass and scree to the summit of Elidir Fawr.

Descend from the summit half L down scree and boulders heading diagonally down the mountainside towards a stream below. Aim to reach the stream at a corner where it meets a fence coming down the mountainside. Cross a ladder stile in the fence (there are two more ladder stiles higher up the hillside) and continue with the stream on the L to eventually cross it by a small footbridge into a farm road. Turn R and follow this down with a quarry to the R *(5)*. Eventually the farm road leaves the stream and swings L. At a sign drop down to the R to a wall, here turn L to a gate by a ruined barn. After the gate, continue down a path to cross a ladder stile and then on to the R of a barn to a farm road. Turn L to a gate to enter a lane. Follow the lane down *(6)* to the main road (A4086) by the chapel in Nant Peris, here turn L and follow the road for 300 yards (275 m) back to the car-park *(7)*.

1 *Old Llanberis*
The name 'Llanberis' is derived from 'Llan Peris' or 'The Church of Peris' and was given originally to the small village around the church dedicated to him, i.e., what is now 'Nant Peris'. The rise of the Dinorwic Quarry at the end of the eighteenth century, however, produced a heavy demand for quarrymen who preferred to live nearer to the quarry, and as a result the centre of population moved down the valley. The old village became known as 'Old Llanberis' and then eventually as 'Nant Peris' or 'The Valley of Peris'.

2 *The Pass of Llanberis*
This is another example of a glacial valley with its characteristic U-shape and truncated spurs. Llyn Peris and Llyn Padarn, just outside the Park, were originally one lake which formed in a trough in the valley floor. They became separate lakes when a bar formed due to silt brought down by a small stream, the Afon Arddu, which flows into the valley from the west.

3 *The Devil's Kitchen* See page 58.

4 *Marchlyn Mawr (The Lake of the Stallion)*
During the rise towards the summit of Elidir Fawr there is a spendid bird's-eye view down to the right of the lake of Marchlyn Mawr, which is now a part of a pumped-storage power station — the largest in Europe — owned and operated by the Central Electricity Generating Board. From the start of construction in 1974, until its official opening ten years later in May 1984 by HRH the Prince of Wales, the entire project cost £450 million to build; although it is expected to pay for itself within eight years. A splendid example of a very profitable and successful state enterprise.

During periods of peak demand or in emergencies, water is allowed to flow from Marchlyn Mawr at nearly 2000 ft (610 m) down tunnels to six turbine-generators situated in a huge machine hall built within the now-disused Dinorwic Quarry. These generate electricity which, after being stepped up from 18,000 to 400,000 volts, is carried by two sets of underground cables to Pentir, near Bangor, about 6 miles

(9.7 km) distant where it is fed into the National Grid. The water passes from the generators into Llyn Peris at about 325 ft (100 m). During periods of low demand at night, the water is pumped back from Llyn Peris to Marchlyn Mawr. The station is able to provide a constant output of 1,680 MW to the National Grid for five hours; to put this into perspective it is over four times the peak electricity demand for the City of Cardiff.

As most of the construction is underground and efforts have been made to landscape some parts of it, the effect on the environment has been limited, but some changes have, of course, been necessary. Marchlyn Mawr, for example, was enlarged by the building of a 1970 ft (600 m) long rock-fill dam and Llyn Peris is now about half again as big as it was before construction began. When the station is operating at maximum output the water levels in the two lakes now rise and fall by considerable amounts — in Marchlyn Mawr by 170 ft (33 m) and in Llyn Peris by 45 ft (14 m) each day!

5 *The Dinorwic Quarry*

The Dinorwic Quarry lies on the western slopes of Elidir Fawr, on the opposite side of Llyn Padarn and Llyn Peris from the town of Llanberis. In its heyday it was one of the two largest slate quarries in the world, employing at its peak in 1898 no less than 3110 men.

The quarry was named after a nearby village, Dinorwic, which in the eighteenth century formed part of the Crown Manor of Vaynol. At that time some small-scale mining of the slate was being undertaken by local quarrymen who paid a small rent in return, but this ceased in 1787 when the Dinorwic Slate Company was formed. By the early years of the nineteenth century the new company had become highly profitable, most of the slates produced being sent by ship from Caernarfon. By 1826 800 men were employed at the quarries and 1600 men by 1848.

The nineteenth century was largely one of continued prosperity for the Dinorwic. Around 1824 a tramway was constructed from the quarries down to the coast, which used horses to haul the trucks, but this was replaced within a few years by a new line employing steam locomotives, the Padarn railway. A private harbour, Port Dinorwic, was constructed at Y Felinheli between Bangor and Caernarfon for the shipment of slates, some of which were carried by the

Y Garn from Glyder Fawr

company's own ships. Many of the slates were sent to the growing British towns by ship and railway, but a lively export trade also developed to Ireland, Germany and many other countries.

As the demand for slate dwindled in this century the fortunes of the Dinorwic changed for the worse; even in the short periods of prosperity after each World War, the quarries were unable to take advantage of the demand due to shortages of labour. In October 1961, the Padarn railway ran its last train and in July 1969, the last quarrymen were laid off.

But there is some future for the Dinorwic. The quarry now houses the machine hall of the largest pumped-storage power station in Europe, the old workshops at Gilfach Ddu have been preserved as a quarrying museum and in summer the Lake Railway at Llanberis runs holidaymakers along the line of the old Padarn railway.

6 *The Copper Mines of North Wales*

The discovery in 1768 of rich copper ore close to the surface at Parys Mountain, 2 miles (3.2 km) from Amlwch in north-east Anglesey, marked the beginning of what was in its day the most important copper mine in Europe. At its height at the end of the eighteenth century some 1200 workers were employed by the industry both in the mine and in the district around. Decline set in, however, early in the nineteenth century and by the middle years production had largely ceased.

Some mining of copper, although on a much smaller scale than at Parys, took place at several other sites in and around Snowdonia. The waste tips seen on the slopes across the valley during the final descent to Nant Peris came from a mine worked from 1763 to the middle of the following century; the Britannia mine in Cwm Dyli was active from at least 1810 to 1926 and other mines were located at Drws-y-Coed in the Nantlle valley, Beddgelert, Nantmor and on the Great Orme near Llandudno. With the exception of Parys Mountain, the copper mines tended to be small and scattered.

7 *The Church of St Peris*

The church at Nant Peris is dedicated to Peris, an early saint of whom little is now known. The long but narrow nave was probably built in the fourteenth or fifteenth centuries, the two transepts were added later and an extension to the east made in the sixteenth century. The latter, which forms the sanctuary and two side chapels, is very unusual and unique in this district. Extensive renovation work has been carried out in recent times.

3·23

Carnedd Llewelyn from Ogwen

STARTING AND FINISHING POINT
Ogwen (115-649603) on the A5 from Capel Curig to Bethesda.
LENGTH
11 miles (17.5 km)
ASCENT
3200 ft (975 m)

A magnificent walk over the southern section of the Carneddau Ridge, which gives extensive views throughout, but particularly over the Ogwen valley from Penyrole-wen. The walk is long but straightforward except for two sections: the steep rise up to Pen y waun-wen and the longer, steeper and more arduous descent of Penyrole-wen at the end of the day. Undoubtedly one of the finest walks in Snowdonia, which includes three of the 3000 ft (914 m) peaks.

Route Description (Maps 39–42)

(1) From Ogwen walk along the A5 towards Bethesda; immediately after the bridge go through a stile on the R. The path goes on the L bank of the lake as far as a stile over a wall; from the wall the path rises up the hillside to the L. After the rise, the path contours along the hillside crossing several small streams and heading towards a farmhouse, Tal-y-llyn-Ogwen. Just before the farmhouse rise L to a stile in a wall, turn R and drop down hill to a farm road (white arrows). Turn L and follow the farm road to the A5, at the end passing by a wooden hut and conifers. Cross the road half R and go through a small gate.

Follow the farm road beyond (The Old Road) *(2) (3)* to the first of two farms, Gwern Gof Uchaf. Pass it to the R over stiles. Continue along to the second farm, Gwern-gof Isaf; pass this to the L across a field. Just beyond the farmhouse, the path leads over a small stream, through a gateway and ahead to the R of a wall. In the middle of a small belt of conifers turn L through a white metal gate and follow a lane to the A5. The cottage to the R is Helyg *(4)*.

Turn L along the A5 *(5)* for 400 yards (365 m) and then R through a gate and up a road. Continue along the road *(6)*, rising slowly through further gates with magnificent views — particularly of Tryfan — to the L. Immediately before a sheep-fold, about 400 yards (365 m) from the last gate, where the road

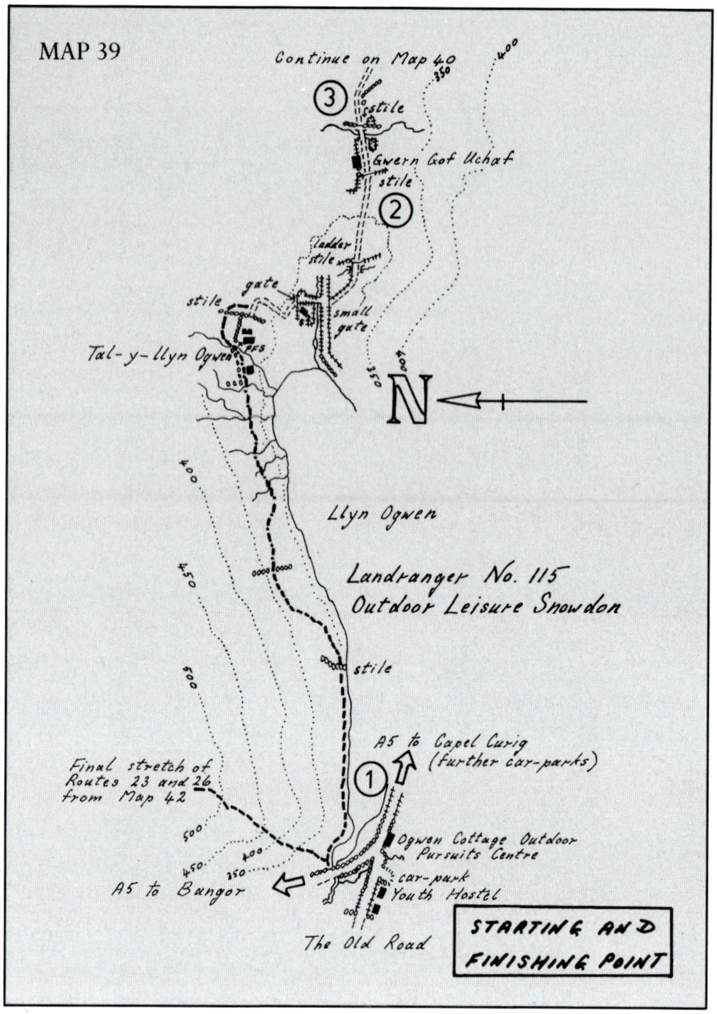

swings L, take the path leaving to the R. This continues in approximately the same direction along the R shore of Ffynnon Llugwy Reservoir; beyond the reservoir rise up a steep slope to reach the top of a ridge at a cairn *(7)*.

Turn L and follow the distinct path along the crest of the narrow ridge, rising eventually to the summit of Carnedd Llewelyn *(8)*. The ridge is narrow at first with a little scrambling but broadens further along beyond the great cliffs of Craig yr Ysfa. From the summit turn L and descend on a faint path to the R of a ruined wall. The path drops to a small col and then continues along the ridge in the same general direction to the summit of Penyrole-wen ($2\frac{3}{4}$ miles, 4.5 km from Carnedd Llewelyn).

To reach the summit of Penyrole-wen, bend L with the path up the final rise keeping to the L side of the ridge, to a cairn which marks the summit. From there it is important to find the best

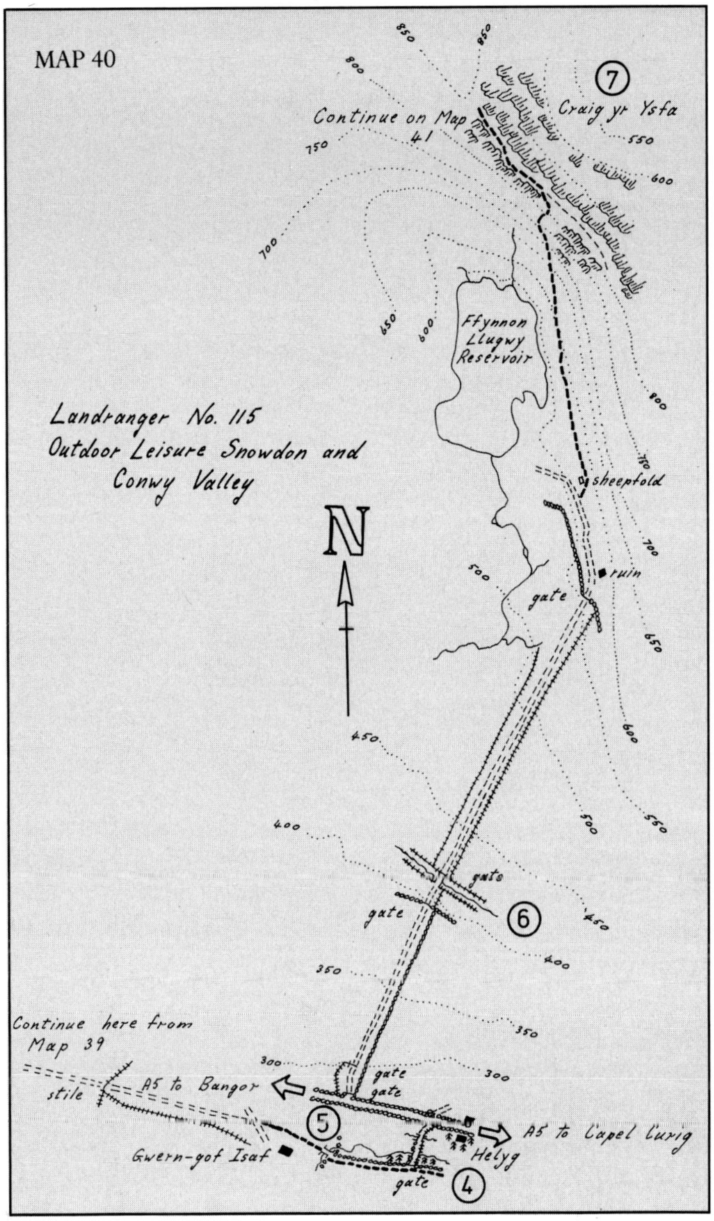

MAP 40

descent point as the summit top is ringed on three sides by very steep slopes and cliffs. Leave the summit to the R from your approach and cross the top, descending slightly to reach a very prominent cairn with stone shelters on the opposite side. From there continue ahead bending slightly L (210° magnetic). After a few yards, you should pick up a very faint path which grows more distinct as you descend, keeping to the L of a cliff edge.

The descent of Penyrole-wen is very long and very steep, particularly in its middle section. The rigours of the descent are matched only by those of the long climb in the opposite

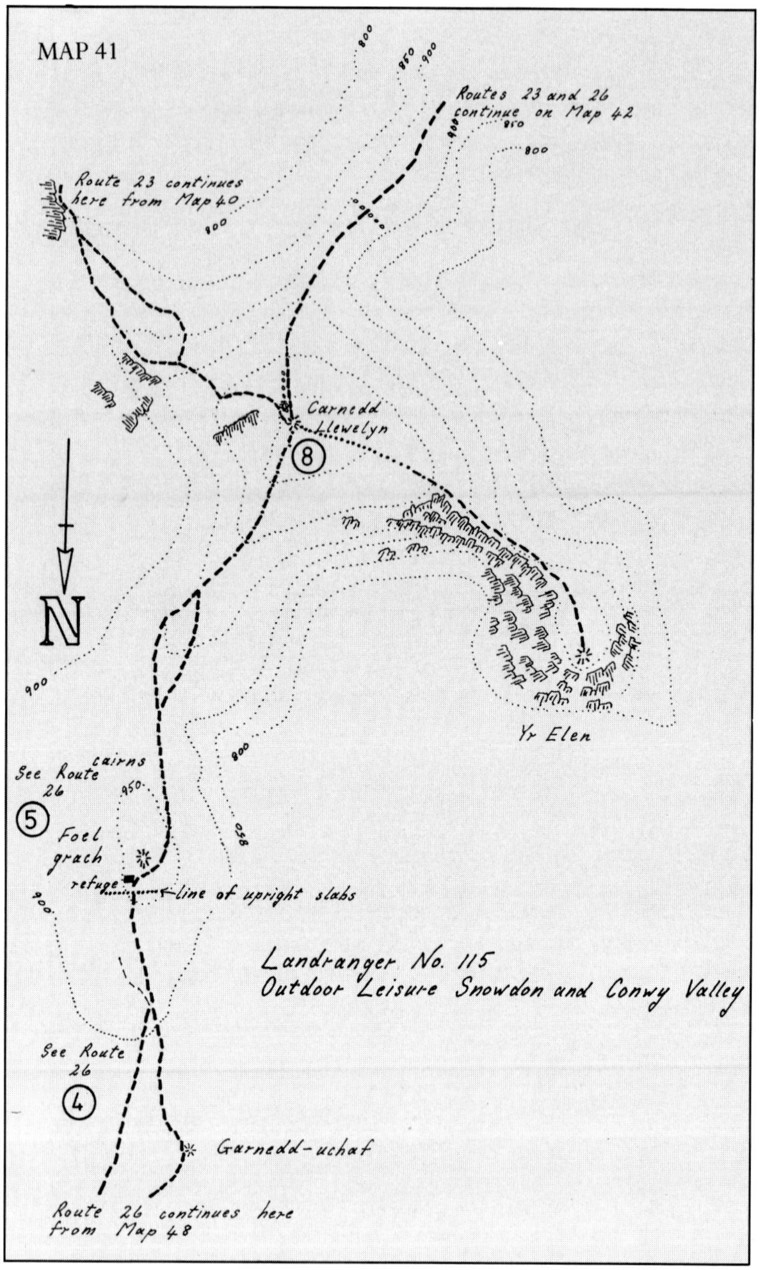

direction, which is generally acknowledged to be one of the most arduous in all Snowdonia.

Eventually, much later, arrive — probably in a considerably weakened condition — at Ogwen where you started earlier.

1 *Aircraft in Snowdonia*

Military aircraft are a prominent feature of the Park, particularly around Ogwen and the Nant Ffrancon Valley. These may be UK or NATO aircraft from any of the airfields

Opposite *Llyn Ogwen*

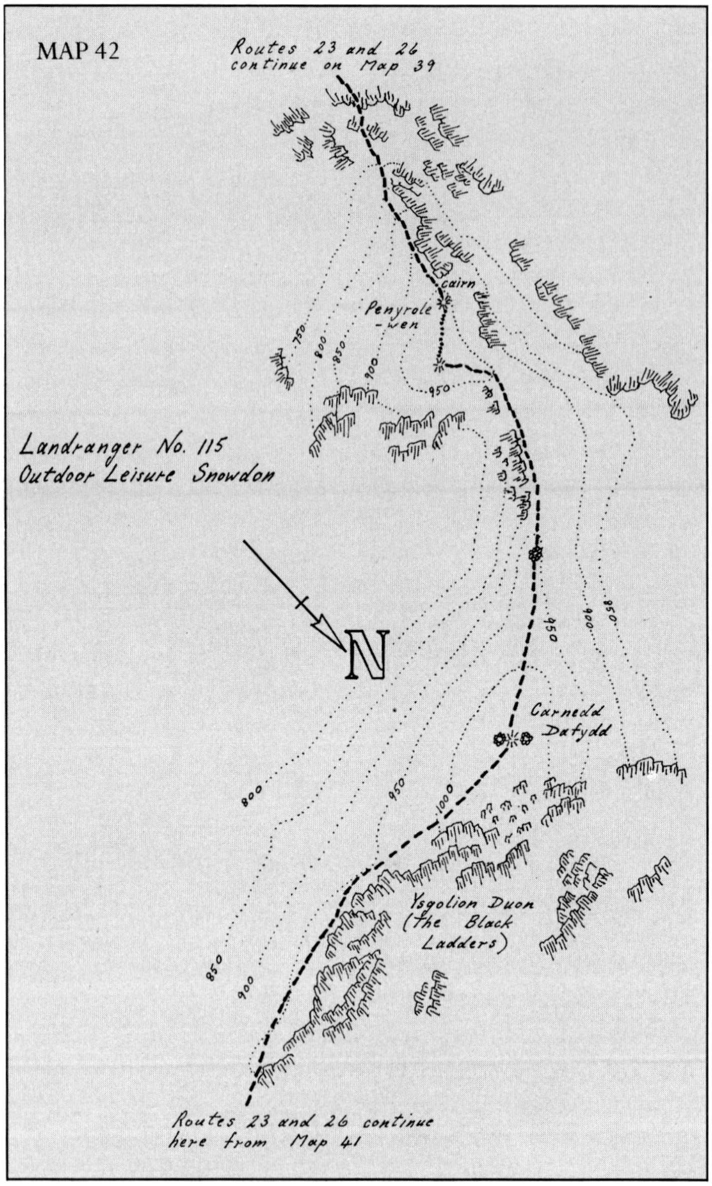

within the UK as flying time into the Park is relatively short. Many come from the Advanced Fast Jet Training School at Royal Air Force Valley, a few miles from Holyhead on Anglesey.

This station was first opened in February 1941 as a base for day and night flights. Today, it is the home of a number of units including 'C' Flight of No. 22 Squadron an operational search and rescue flight, the Search and Rescue Training Unit (SARTU) which trains helicopter pilots, navigators and winchmen to carry out search and rescue duties, and the No. 4 Flying Training School for fast jet pilots. The latter unit has operated the British Aerospace Hawk T1 since 1976, and these red and white training aircraft may be frequently seen around the Park.

2 *The Old Road*

The main obstacle to road construction through the Nant Ffrancon Valley lies at the western end of Llyn Ogwen where the Afon Ogwen plunges over a rock cliff over 200 ft (60 m) high. The first road through the valley to surmount this step was built in 1791 by Lord Penrhyn, owner of the Penrhyn Quarry at Bethesda, to reach his lands at Capel Curig with the intention of developing them for the tourist trade. The Penrhyn road was soon supplanted by a turnpike built in 1805 and later by a second and much superior turnpike built by Thomas Telford. The Old Road runs roughly parallel with the present A5 but on the opposite side of the valley and of the Afon Ogwen, remaining reasonably level at around the 725 ft (220 m) contour, to a short distance beyond Pentre where it begins to climb. Its route coincides with that of the A5 around Llyn Ogwen, but from there it again takes a more southerly route on the opposite side of the stream as far as Capel Curig, which it enters over a single span stone bridge over the Afon Llugwy.

3 *Telford's Turnpike*

The A5, running from Bethesda to Capel Curig through the valley of the Nant Ffrancon and surmounting the steep rise by the Rhaeadr Ogwen at an easy gradient of 1 in 22, stands as a memorial to the genius of one man, Thomas Telford, probably the greatest builder of canals, roads and bridges during the years of the Industrial Revolution.

Telford was born in 1757, the only son of a humble shepherd of the border region of Eskdale in eastern Dumfries and Galloway; when he died in 1834 he was laid to rest among the famous in the nave of Westminster Abbey. The Birmingham and Liverpool Junction Canal, the Caledonian Canal, the Holyhead Road and the bridges at Conwy and over the Menai Straits were but the greatest of his many achievements.

In addition to the road built by Lord Penrhyn up the Nant Ffrancon, a turnpike had been constructed by 1805 to reach the harbour at Holyhead, which serviced the cross-channel boats to Ireland. Although initially successful, shortage of money, both in the building and in the maintenance, soon produced such a deterioration in the state of the road that passage became extremely difficult and at times impossible, and an attempt to run the mail coach along it proved a failure.

Largely as a result of the influence of two Irish Members of Parliament, John Foster, Chancellor of the Irish Exchequer, and later Henry Parnell, member for Queen's County, Telford was commissioned to survey the route. A preliminary report was completed in 1811 and a detailed one in 1817. The work itself lasted for fifteen years, although a through route was established by 1826 with the opening of the bridge over the Menai Straits.

4 *Helyg*

The cottage of Helyg below the cliffs of Gallt yr Ogof about 2½ miles (4 km) out of Capel Curig on the Bangor Road was visited in 1854 by George Borrow who stopped there for a drink of water on a long walk of 34 miles (55 km) from Cerrig-y-Drudion to Bangor, which he covered in a single day. In his book, *Wild Wales, Its People, Language and Scenery*, published in 1862, which has become a classic and still sells well today, he described it as 'a wretched hovel'.

It was derelict and unoccupied when acquired by the Climbers' Club in 1925, opening as a club hut on 30 October. Under the pressure of increasing use it was rebuilt and extended in 1933.

5 *Tryfan from Helyg*

A magnificent view of the east face of Tryfan is obtained from the road by Helyg Cottage. The two objects close together on the summit are often mistaken for climbers, but are in fact two stone blocks about 6 ft (2 m) high, called Adam and Eve. The Heather Terrace lower down the East Face is used by climbers to reach the base of some rock climbs, whilst the usual walkers' route traverses the peak more or less along the skyline of the mountain.

6 *The Leat*

The watercourse crossed about ½ mile (0.8 km) from the road is a man-made leat that diverts water from the high ground above into Llyn Cowlyd. From Llyn Cowlyd the water is taken by pipeline to the power station at Dolgarrog.

7 *Craig yr Ysfa*

A great crag in the Carneddau on the eastern slopes of Carnedd Llewelyn. The crag was late in being explored by rock climbers due to its remote situation, but now has numerous routes. The first climbing hut in Britain was established below the crag in Cwm Eigiau by the Rucksack Club in 1912.

8 *Carnedd Llewelyn and Carnedd Dafydd*

These are the two highest peaks in the range of mountains

View SE from the rise to Ffynnon Llugwy Reservoir

between the Nant Ffrancon and the sea, which give the name to the entire range. The peaks are named after Llewelyn the Last who was recognized as Prince of all Wales by the Treaty of Montgomery in 1267 and his brother Dafydd (or David) who attempted to assume that title after his brother's death. Llewelyn was the last native Prince of Wales.

3·24

THE SNOWDON HORSESHOE

STARTING AND FINISHING POINT
Pen-y-Pass (115-647557)
LENGTH
$7\frac{1}{2}$ miles (12 km)
ASCENT
3250 ft (990 m)

The finest ridge walk south of the Black Cuillin of Skye. From Pen-y-Pass, a rough path leads to a steep scramble up the rock peak of Crib-goch. This is followed by a magnificent, but exposed, traverse along a rock 'knife edge' above deep and impressive cymoedd until the easier ground of Crib-y-ddysgl and Yr Wyddfa is reached. From the main summit, a steep descent of rocky and scree-strewn slopes lead to the second arm of the horseshoe, the arête of Y Lliwedd. The finish is along an easy track back to the starting point. The route is not long, but involves a considerable amount of scrambling along high and exposed ridges above spectacular cliffs and requires care. In snow or ice conditions it should be attempted only by experienced mountaineers.

ROUTE DESCRIPTION (Maps 43–45, 30 — see also page 124)

Starting in the car park at Pen-y-Pass with your back towards the hostel *(1)* take the track which leaves the far R-hand corner. This is the Pyg Track *(2)*, which goes behind the restaurant and through a wall gap. No difficulty should be found in following this rough but well-marked path, which rises gradually and diagonally up the hillside for about $\frac{3}{4}$ mile (1.2 km) before it steepens and then swings to the L (cairns). The path emerges upon a small col, Bwlch y Moch. On a clear day there are glorious views ahead down into Cwm Dyli and across to the peaks of the horseshoe, Yr Wyddfa and Y Lliwedd, which will be crossed later in the day.

Two paths leave the col to the R. The L-hand one is the continuation of the Pyg Track whilst the R-hand one, which rises immediately, leads to the Horseshoe (there is a slab marker at the start). Take the Horseshoe path which rises slowly at first, but later more steeply. Ahead rises the great rock peak of Crib-goch. Climb this directly, selecting the best route up the rocks,

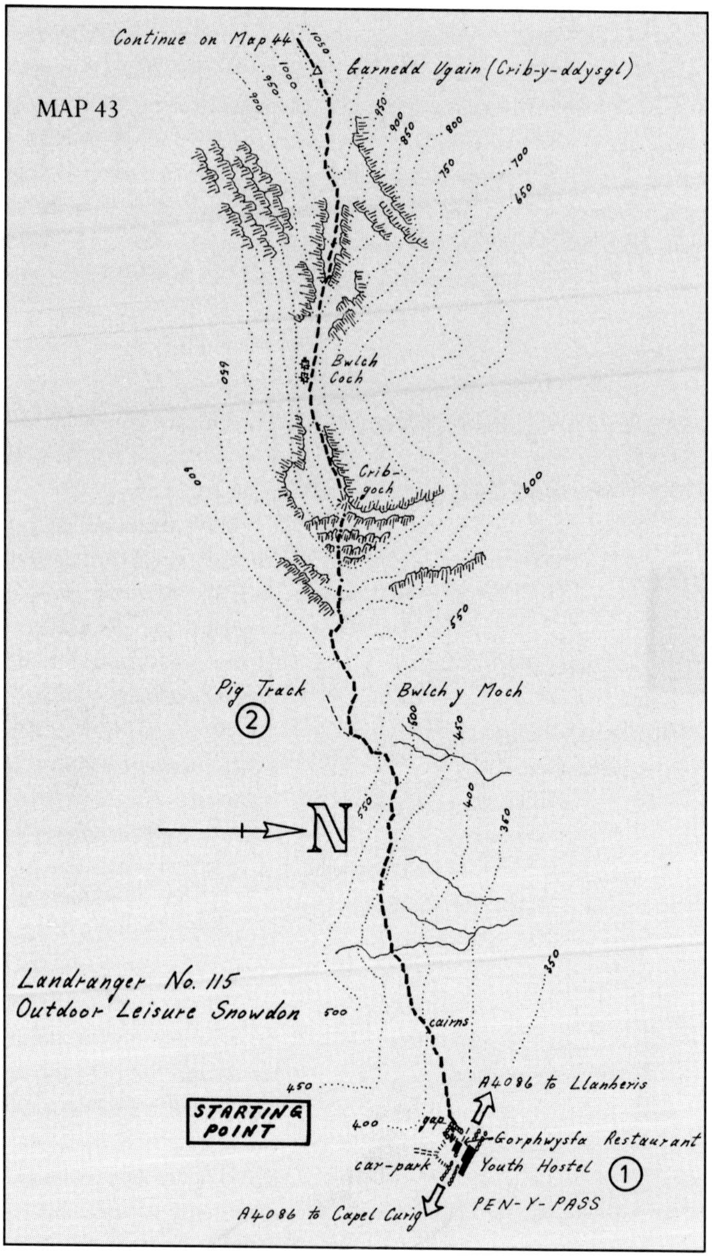

It will be necessary to use hands for balance, particularly on the upper sections. There is a rise of about 900–1000 ft (275–300 m) from the col to the summit.

The summit of Crib-goch is one of the most magnificent situations in Snowdonia. Steep rocky slopes fall away in every direction except where the summit is joined by the long undulating arête of the Horseshoe.

Opposite *Rock-work on the Snowdon Horseshoe near Crib-goch*

The route along the arête is now obvious. It is possible to keep on the crest throughout, but many walkers will find it

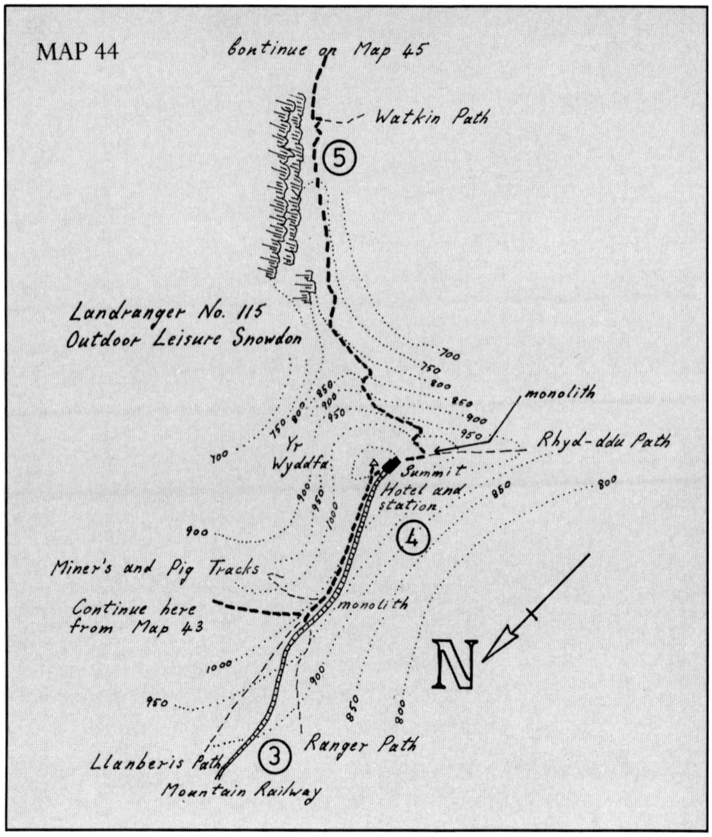

easier to by-pass some of the more difficult sections to the L. Great care is needed here as the drops are considerable, particularly to the right. After about ¼ mile (400 m) the grassy col of Bwlch Coch (enclosures) will be reached and after about 1 mile (1.6 km) the OS pillar on Crib-y-ddysgl. From Bwlch Coch keep more or less along the crest of the ridge and not across the scree slopes down to the L. Beyond, continue along a path, descending easily to reach the Bwlch Glas (rock monolith) and the track of the railway *(3)*. Turn L and follow the railway up to the summit. The summit cairn is to the L of the hotel building *(4)*.

Leave the hotel from the opposite end, i.e. from the small walled enclosure, and continue ahead on a path down a ridge. Lower down at a rock monolith, turn L to the edge and descend steeply on a shattered path down a huge and loose slope gradually slanting to the L, to reach the col, Bwlch-y-Saethau *(5)*. The path then continues along level ground for about ⅝ mile (1 km) across the col. At a path junction by a large cairn (Bwlch Ciliau), take the L-hand path, which rises steeply to the first peak of Y Lliwedd.

The route traverses the two peaks of Y Lliwedd (West and

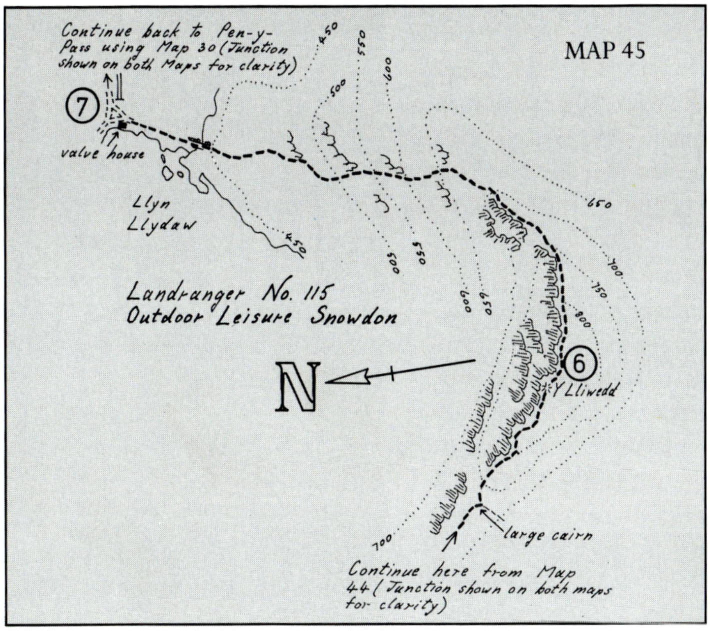

The Snowdon Mountain Railway

East) below, dropping down to the lower height of Lliwedd Bach. Great care is needed throughout the traverse of Y Lliwedd, as the route keeps close to the lip of a tremendous precipice, the highest in Wales, which plunges on the L into the depths of Cwm Dyli *(6)*. Continue descending, following the cliff edge, until a prominent cairn on a grassy area is reached and the path falls away to the L down a steep slope. Descend this to reach the Miners' Track *(7)* near to the shore of Llyn Llydaw. Turn R along the track and continue easily — both physically and mentally now that all difficulties are behind you — for about 1¼ miles (2 km) back to Pen-y-Pass.

1 Gorphwysfa Hotel, Pen-y-Pass

The valley roads of North Wales were built in the period between 1805 and 1830, the last important construction being that over the Llanberis Pass to link Capel Curig with Nant Peris. Prior to that, the pass could only be crossed by a rocky path, which, according to James Bransby who visited the area, was 'irregular and rough and full of quagmires'.

A few years after the road was constructed, a small inn was built for the benefit of travellers in a sheltered position at the top of the pass at a height of 1170 ft (357 m). Although providing a living for its tenants, it tended, however, to be overshadowed by the Pen-y-Gwryd Hotel established earlier and lower down in the valley about 1 mile (1.6 km) away. This state of affairs changed in 1900 when the inn was taken over by a great personality, Owen Rawson Owen, who remained its tenant until his death at the age of eighty-five in 1962. The original inn was also replaced by a much larger building, the Gorphwysfa Hotel, at the turn of the century. In the years that followed, the hotel became the meeting place of a close group of climbers, led by the famous Geoffrey Winthrop Young, and mainly from a public school background, who pioneered routes up the great crags of the district in the first great wave of exploration.

Later its importance declined as climbing clubs acquired their own huts and as a new type of climber, of working class origin, took over the leadership in the hills. It was typical of the times that the Gorphwysfa Hotel became a Youth Hostel in 1967. But, in its day, it made a valuable contribution to Welsh climbing. To remind us of this, two slate tablets have been placed in the front porch which faces out towards Crib-goch and Snowdon: the first to the memory of 'Owen Rawson Owen, 1877–1962, Host of Pen-y-Pass for 60 years', and the second to 'Geoffrey Winthrop Young, 1876–1958, Mountaineer and Poet'.

2 *The Pig or Pyg Track*

The path which runs from Pen-y-Pass around the southern slopes of Crib-goch to the summit of Snowdon is marked on the Outdoor Leisure map as the Pig Track and on the 1:50 000 map as the Pyg Track. The former name may be derived from Bwlch y Moch, The Pass of the Pigs, through which the path leads, although there is some doubt if this translation is correct. The alternative spelling was given to it by climbers from the Pen-y-Gwryd Hotel and was derived from the initials of the hotel's name.

3 *The Snowdon Mountain Railway*

The summit of Snowdon is visited by more people than any other mountain top in the British Isles. This has been the case for far longer than most would imagine. One writer in 1857, for example, commented that 'North Wales is thronged this summer by tourists — Snowdon is ascended by everyone because it is the highest top'.

The commercial attractions of a mountain railway were quickly realized, but two early attempts in the 1870s to launch schemes were unsuccessful, due mainly to the efforts of a local landowner, George Assheton-Smith. A third attempt in 1894, however, was successful and the construction began that year, being completed in about fourteen months.

Y Lliwedd and Llyn Llydaw

The public opening on Easter Monday, 1896 was marred unfortunately by the only major accident — and fatality — to occur on the line. Two trains, one following soon after the other along the same track, had safely reached the summit. On the descent, however, the leading engine mounted the track and ran out of control, eventually leaving the track at a bend and crashing down the steep slopes of the mountain — to the immense discomfiture of several walkers and a climber, who had the unique experience of observing the passage of the engine at close quarters. The second train, unaware of the accident, crashed into the back of the stationary carriages, fortunately now empty. Incredibly, there was only one death — a passenger who leapt from the moving coach and broke his legs. He died later in hospital from his injury.

Today, seven steam and two diesel locomotives are used, pushing single carriages up the $4\frac{3}{4}$ miles (7.5 km) of single track from Llanberis to the top of Yr Wyddfa. The average gradient is 1 in 7.8, but there are some stretches as steep as $1{:}5\frac{1}{2}$. At these steep gradients the normal method of working, which relies upon the grip between smooth wheels and rail, is not practicable, and the Abt system (named after Dr Roman Abt, who first used this system in the Harz mountains) is employed, where pinions on the engine make contact with a rack, which consists of two rows of teeth laid in the centre between the rails. The steam engines were manufactured by the Swiss Locomotive and Machine Co. of Winterthur and are fired by coal, their plumes of smoke being familiar sights on Snowdon. Each locomotive is fitted with two separate braking systems — hand and steam — to ensure complete safety. The diesel locomotives are built to a completely modern design and were manufactured by Hunslet of Leeds using 320 HP Rolls Royce engines.

4 *The Summit Hotel*

There have been buildings on the summit of Snowdon for over 150 years, since 1820 when a small hut was constructed from local stone. This hut and subsequent buildings were maintained by professional guides who catered for the many visitors climbing the mountain from Llanberis. By the middle of the century, the ascent of the highest mountain was almost a requirement for Victorian holiday-makers in the area and the provision of food and drink was a highly profitable business. By 1890 a wooden building known as Roberts and Owens Bazaar, provided 'well aired beds, ham and eggs and choice beverages' for visitors.

The first Summit Hotel, owned by the Railway Company, was built in 1897. The present building was constructed in

1934 and offered beds and meals until the end of 1942, when it was occupied by the Air Ministry, and then the Admiralty and War Department in turn, for secret development work. At present, the building is open from late spring to early October for light refreshments; out of season it is heavily shuttered against intruders. It was purchased by the Snowdonia National Park Authority in 1983, although the catering arrangements are continued by the Snowdon Mountain Railway Company. The building was re-opened by Mr Wyn Roberts, Under Secretary of State for Wales, at an official ceremony on 12th September 1988 after being completely refurbished inside and out.

5 *Bwlch-y-Saethau*

According to Welsh legend, a battle was fought here in the sixth century between King Arthur and his nephew, Medrod or Modred. Arthur is supposed to have died in the battle and been buried on the pass under a huge cairn. The pass has therefore become known by this name, which is translated as the Pass of the Arrows. It is said that his followers still sleep in a great cave on the face of Y Lliwedd awaiting a further call upon their services.

6 *Y Lliwedd*

The northern face of Y Lliwedd is a huge cliff over 1000 ft (300 m) in height. It featured prominently in the early days of British rock climbing when it attracted some of the leading climbers of the day: J. M. A. Thomson, A. W. Andrews, Oscar Eckenstein, Marcus Heywood, Geoffrey Winthrop Young and George Leigh Mallory of Everest. It was the subject of the first Welsh climbers' guidebook *The Climbs on Lliwedd* written by Thomson and Andrews, which provoked a short poem:

> The climber goeth forth to climb on Lliwedd,
> And seeketh him a way where man hath trod,
> But which of all the thousand routes he doeth
> Is known only to Andrews and to Thomson.

Sadly, today, the great face of Y Lliwedd is neglected by modern climbers, who have found harder adversaries elsewhere.

7 *The Miners' Track*

A broad and well-maintained track running from Pen-y-Pass into Cwm Dyli, built in 1856 for the Britannia Copper Mine.

3·25

The Idwal Skyline

STARTING AND FINISHING POINT
Ogwen (115-649603), on the A5 from Capel Curig to Bethesda.
LENGTH
6 miles (9.5 km).
Alternative 7 miles (11 km)
ASCENT
3100 ft (945 m).
Alternative 4000 ft (1220 m)

This is the most exciting route in Snowdonia after the Snowdon Horseshoe. It involves two considerable stretches of scrambling, the North Ridge of Tryfan and Bristly Ridge on Glyder Fach and these stretches make it a route for the experienced only. The majority of walkers will find that the ascent of Bristly Ridge is the hardest section described in this book. The route is so named because it traverses the skyline of peaks around Llyn Idwal.

Route Description (Maps 46, 15, 16, 37 — see also pages 81, 82 and 143).

From Ogwen walk along the main road (A5) towards Capel Curig. Continue to the furthest lay-by on the R (at the time of writing this is the fifth) and turn R through a small gate. At this

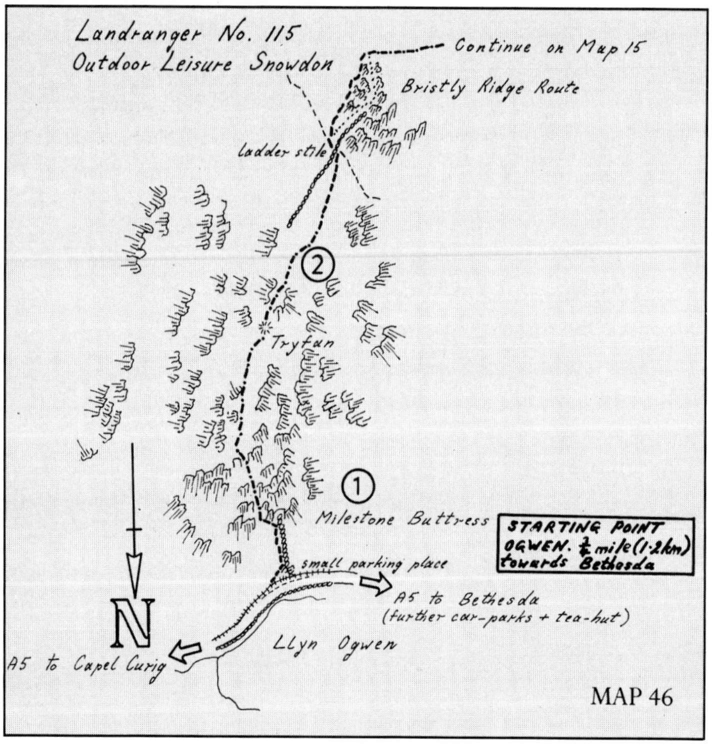

MAP 46

Tryfan and Bristly Ridge

point a wall comes down the hillside from the prominent cliff at the base of Tryfan to meet the road fence. Follow a path up the hillside towards the cliff with the wall on the R. Just before the wall ends at the cliff face *(1)*, turn L to leave it and climb up a shallow boulder-strewn groove between the rock face on the R and smaller rocks on the L. Eventually reach the crest of the ridge.

Here, turn half R and ascend the ridge (i.e. the North Ridge) to the summit of Tryfan. A path will be found with some cairns for much of the way and the rock is well marked with the passage of many boots, but this is a long scramble and hands will have to be used constantly; there is also a fair degree of exposure particularly in the upper reaches. The huge slab pointing out from the mountain along the way is called the 'Cannon'. The route finishes by the two upright pillars on the summit *(2)*.

Cross the summit and continue down the South Ridge ahead, selecting the best route for descent around small crags and boulders. Eventually curve round to the L to reach the wall on the Bwlch Tryfan; cross this at a ladder stile. Continue to the far side of the col with the wall on the R towards some rocks ahead (this is Bristly Ridge). Choosing a convenient point, climb the

ALTERNATIVE:

The full Idwal Skyline Walk also takes in the summit of Y Garn. For this, after the descent from Glyder Fawr, go round the R shore of Llyn y Cŵn to pick up a path that leads ahead in the same direction towards Y Garn, at first over grassy slopes and later over scree. Reach the summit cairn. (A fence has been erected between Llyn y Cŵn and Y Garn, cross this at a stile.)

The cirque to the R of the summit is Cwm Clyd. Continue beyond the summit and then descend to the R from the summit ridge down the steep ridge, which is the far arm of the cwm. The clear path descends to the northern end of Llyn Idwal. Go round the L shore of the lake to a gate. From the gate take the very clear path which descends to Ogwen.

rocks to reach the crest and scramble up the ridge to the L to reach the top. Again, considerable care is needed in the ascent as some of the drops are considerable.

For the section from the top of Bristly Ridge to Ogwen, follow Route 13 (Maps 15 and 16).

1 *The Milestone Buttress*
The prominent cliff on the lower point of the north ridge of Tryfan, directly above the start of the Idwal Skyline Walk, acquired its name because it lay above the tenth milestone from Bangor along the road to Capel Curig. It was first climbed by Owen Glynne Jones and the Abraham brothers, George Dixon and Ashley Perry, in 1899 but is now regarded as a fairly easy training ground for beginners.

2 *Adam and Eve*
These are the names given to the two rock pillars about 6 ft (2 m) high on the summit of Tryfan. There is an old tradition amongst climbers and walkers that anyone who steps from the top of one pillar to the other receives the Freedom of Tryfan. A fair drop on one side, however, lends a certain element of danger to this venture!

Tryfan and the Ogwen Valley. The peak to the right is Penyrole-wen

3·26

THE GREAT RIDGE OF THE CARNEDDAU

STARTING POINT
Bontnewydd (115-663720). On A55 from Bangor to Conwy turn R at Aber on minor road and follow signs to Aber Falls. Start where road turns L over bridge. Cars should be left at the Forestry Commission car-park over the bridge and not at the mountain gate further along.
FINISHING POINT
Ogwen (115-649605)
LENGTH
11 miles (17.5 km). (12½ miles (20 km) with Yr Elen)
ASCENT
4350 ft (1325 m). (5000 ft (1525 m) with Yr Elen)

The Carneddau summits, in a continuous ridge from the north coast of Wales to the Ogwen Valley, offer one of the finest high-level walks in the Park. There are several possible approach routes from the north, but the one chosen is from Aber by Llyn Anafon to reach the ridge at Drum. The ridge is then followed in a general SW direction over a series of summits, including Carnedd Llewelyn, the third highest mountain in the Park, to the final one of Penyrole-wen overlooking Ogwen. Magnificent and very extensive views range from Puffin Island in the north to Snowdon and the southern peaks of the Park to the south. The walking is fairly straightforward over grass or bare scree slopes, except for the final descent to Ogwen, which is very steep and very arduous. The route reaches the summits of five of the three thousanders (or six if Yr Elen is included).

ROUTE DESCRIPTION (Maps 47, 48, 41, 42, 39 — see also pages 152, 154 and 150)

Cross the bridge and walk up the road *(1)*, eventually reaching a gate where the metalled road ends. Go through the gate and up the farm road to a cross track *(2) (3)*; continue in the same direction on a track up the hillside to a higher farm road where you turn R. Follow this farm road up a valley with a stream to the R to reach a lake, Llyn Anafon. Where the track bends R to the lake, leave it to the L and climb up a steep slope (no path) to the crest of the ridge near to the summit of Drum.

Turn R along the ridge. The ridge top is marked by a fence or a wall for 1½ miles (2.4 km) to beyond Foel-fras. Where these end continue along the ridge over the summits of Garnedd-uchaf *(4)* and Foel grach (passing the refuge *(5)* just before the summit — see important note page 177) to Carnedd Llewelyn.

A detour can be made from Carnedd Llewelyn to Yr Elen, but this will involve about 1½ miles (2.4 km) of further walking. If you decide to do this, turn R at the summit of Carnedd

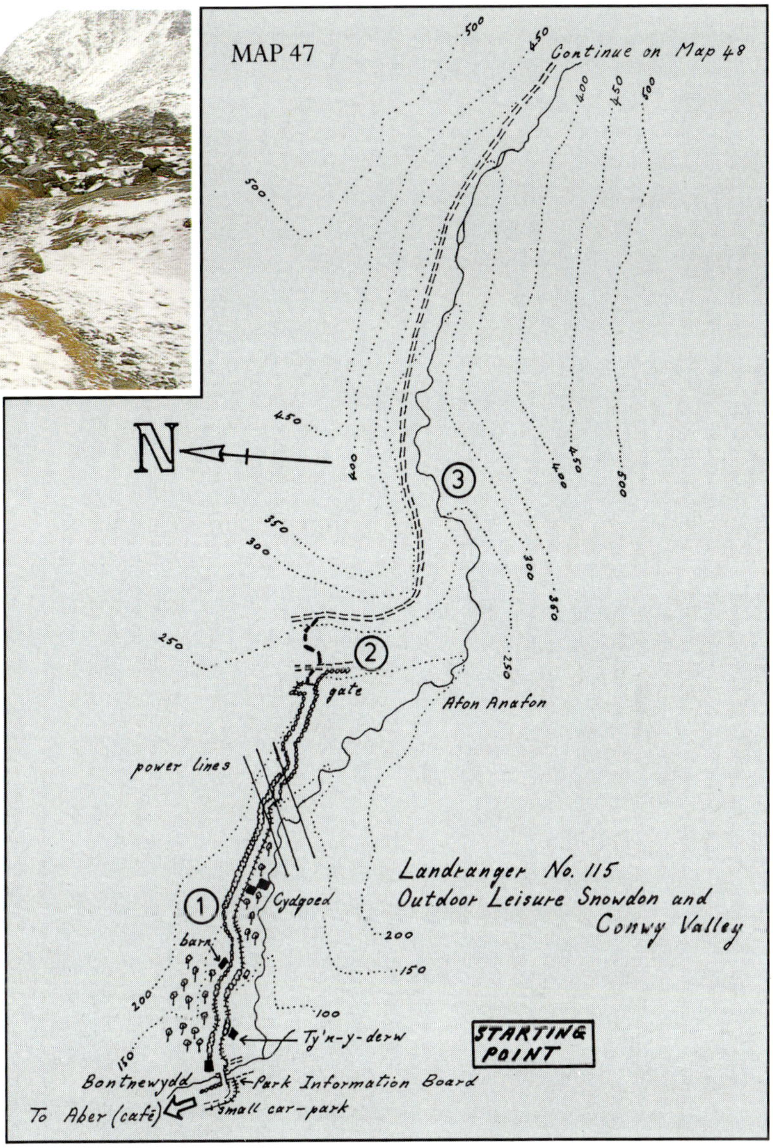

Llewelyn and cross the top of the mountain to the far side; descend on a path to a narrow ridge and cross, curving slightly R to the summit of Yr Elen (there are cliffs to the R). Return to Carnedd Llewelyn by the same route.

See Route 23 for the remainder of the way to Ogwen.

1 *The Roman Road*

A Roman road from the auxiliary fort of Kanovium at Caerhun on the west bank of the Afon Conwy to the fort of Segontium at Caernarfon ran over the Bwlch y Ddeufaen (The Pass of Two Stones) and down the valley of the Afon Anafon, coinciding with the minor road used at the start of

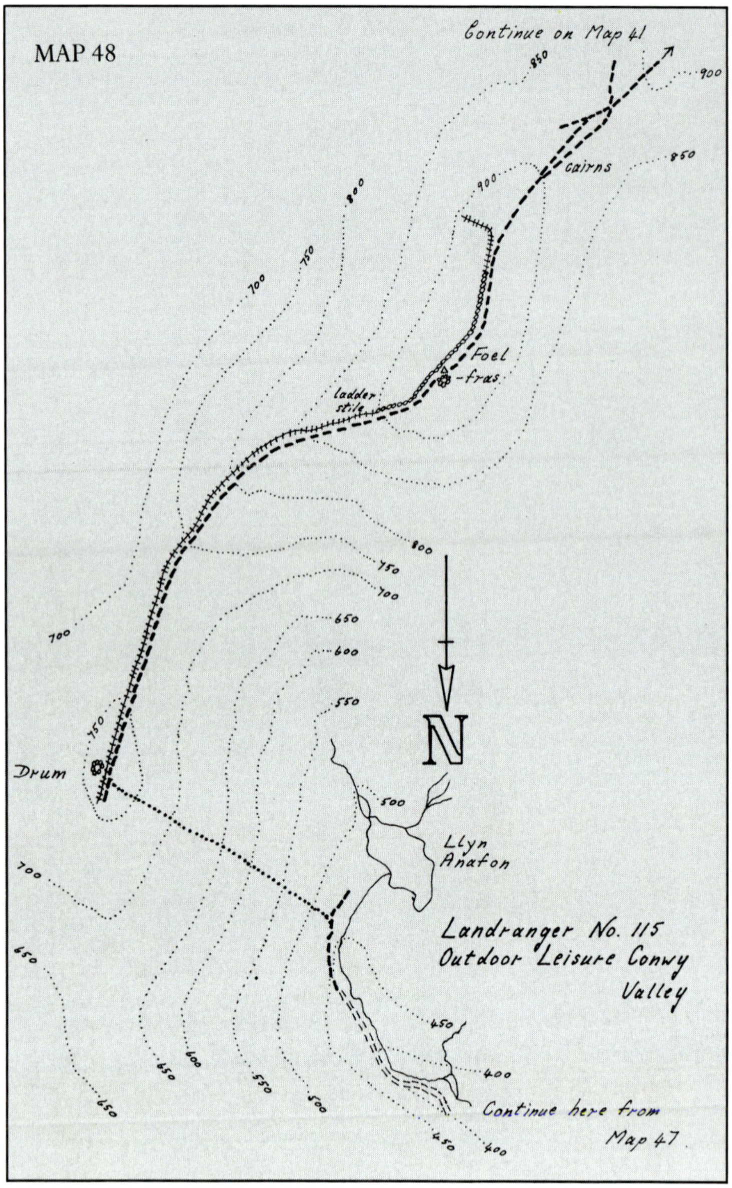

Route 26. This provided a better route than could be found along the coast, where the hill of Penmaen Mawr provided a difficult obstacle. The road is now a track well-marked throughout but, unfortunately from the scenic point of view, accompanied by rows of pylons. The two stones themselves are prehistoric monoliths. Kanovium was at the junction of two important roads; the first described above from Caernarfon to Chester, and Sarn Helen running south.

The approach to the Carneddau by Afon Anafon

2 *The National Trust in North Wales*

The large area of wild country to the west of the main ridge of the Carneddau summits from near Aber to the Nant Ffrancon and Llyn Ogwen, plus the summits to the south from Foel-goch to Gallt yr Ogof, belong to the National Trust. This area is the Carneddau section of the Ysbyty Estate, its 15,860 acres (6419 ha) including nine of the fourteen peaks over 3000 ft (914 m) within the Park. Access is permitted throughout the area except for parts of the Nant Ffrancon and Ogwen Valleys, where public footpaths must be used.

3 *Motor Cycles in the Carneddau*

There have recently been disturbing reports of the increasing use of motor cycles and four wheel drive vehicles in the upland areas of the Park. They have no right to be there, as the driving or riding of any vehicle off the Highway without lawful authority constitutes an offence under Section 36 of the 1972 Road Traffic Act. Apart from this, the use of such vehicles causes disturbance to livestock and the public as well as damage to the environment. Concern for this, therefore, has rightly been shown by the Snowdonia National Park Authority, Nature Conservancy Council, National Trust, National Farmers' Union and local landowners. Any sighting, which can be verified by factual evidence, e.g. details of registration numbers, time, place, etc. should be reported to the nearest police station.

4 *The Eigiau Dam and the Disaster at Dolgarrog*

Llyn Eigiau and Coedty Reservoir to the east of the main ridge were the scene in 1925 of a major dam disaster, which resulted in the deaths of sixteen people in the village of Dolgarrog in the Conwy Valley. The disaster began at 9.15 on the evening of 2 November, when water broke through the clay layer beneath the Eigiau Dam. The escaping water poured down the Afon Porth-llwyd into the Coedty Reservoir which rapidly filled, leading in turn to a complete and sudden collapse of its own dam. A wall of water descended upon Dolgarrog causing extensive damage. The fault lay in the unsatisfactory foundations of the Eigiau Dam, probably coupled with the unusually dry summer previously, which had caused the bed to be exposed with the formation of deep shrinkage cracks.

5 *The Foel grach Refuge* (115-689659)

The refuge, which lies a short distance north of the summit cairn of Foel grach, was erected during the summer months of 1964. When erected it was a small but sturdy building, built from local slabs of stone mortared together and with a

Sheepfolds

roof of sheet iron held down with boulders against the violence of winter storms. Inside were two plain benches. It was built by some local walkers and climbers who gave up their free time to erect the refuge where they thought it would be most needed, at a remote spot near to the centre of the Carneddau, and others since then have been grateful for their efforts. Unfortunately, some visitors saw fit to scratch their initials on the commemorative tablet on the wall of the refuge and to enter obscene remarks into the visitors' book; it was also on occasions used as a bothy by some walkers who were, no doubt, perfectly able to walk on to accommodation in the valleys below. In 1988, partly for these reasons, the roof, door and shutter were removed and a small sheet metal shelter of reduced capacity erected within the walls. *At the moment the future of the refuge is under consideration and it is possible that it may be removed altogether.*

Twelve upright slabs of rock have been placed at intervals of about fifteen to twenty paces each, across the ridge just north of the refuge to aid its location.

4·27

The Welsh 1000 Metres

STARTING POINT
Bethania (115-627506), 3 miles (5 km) from Beddgelert along the road (A498) towards Capel Curig.
FINISHING POINT
Aber (115-655728), 4 miles (6.5 km) from Llandegai on the road (A55) from Bangor to Conwy.
LENGTH
22 miles (35 km)
ASCENT
9600 ft (2925 m)

Although there are fourteen summits over 3000 ft (914 m) in North Wales, only four of them are over 3280 ft (1000 metres), two on Snowdon and two in the Carneddau. Any walk linking these summits together must therefore cross the Glyder-Elidir Fawr ridge at some convenient point. There is no fixed route for the Welsh 1000 metres, although most people probably start from Pen-y-Pass. The route described starts from Bethania and includes the Watkin Path, as the intention is not to cut the distance to an absolute minimum, but to produce a route of superlative quality bringing in the very best of the scenery in the Snowdonia National Park. The route described is very long and very arduous, and as a single expedition is likely to be well beyond the powers of most; there is no reason, however, why it should not be completed in a three-day expedition using Youth Hostels, campsites along the way or convenient transport between the sections.

The walk may be divided into three convenient stages:
Bethania to Pen-y-Pass 7 miles (11 km) 3860 ft (1175 m)
Pen-y-Pass to Ogwen 4 miles (6.5 km) 2090 ft (640 m)
Ogwen to Aber 11 miles (17.5 km) 3650 ft (1110 m)

Route Description (Map references follow in main text)

From Bethania follow the Watkin Path to the summit of Snowdon — see Route 19 for maps and route description. Continue from the station end of the Summit Hotel and follow the path down by the railway track to the Bwlch Glas. Just beyond the rock monolith marking the top of the zig-zags on the Miners' Track, take the path to the R which leads to Crib-y-ddysgl and on to Crib-goch over the arm of the Snowdon Horseshoe. From Crib-goch, continue in roughly the same direction, descending steeply down the rocky face eventually reaching Bwlch y Moch; here a path (the Pyg Track) goes down to the L. Follow this to Pen-y-Pass (for the map of this, see

Opposite *Waterfalls in Cwm Llan by the Watkin Path*

Route 24 which goes in the opposite direction).

At Pen-y-Pass, cross the road and go over the ladder stile in the wall to the L of the Youth Hostel. Follow this path to the summit of Glyder Fawr. For the descent from Glyder Fawr to Ogwen by Llyn Idwal see Route 13.

Reach the main road at Ogwen and turn L over the bridge. Immediately after the bridge go through a stile to the R. Follow the path which strikes up the steep and very rough face of Penyrole-wen. From the summit, the route leads along the ridge as far as Drum. From Drum descend to the L from the ridge to reach a rough farm road to the R of Llyn Anafon, turn R along it. This eventually curves R and later bends L under power lines to reach the end of a minor road. Continue down this road to cross a bridge (Bontnewydd) and on to Aber. (For the map from Ogwen to Aber see Route 26 which is done in the opposite direction.)

The face of Penyrole-wen from Cwm Idwal

4·28

The Welsh Three Thousands

STARTING POINT
Bethania (115-627506), 3 miles (5 km) from Beddgelert along the road (A498) towards Capel Curig.
FINISHING POINT
Aber (115-655728), 4 miles (6.5 km) from Llandegai on the coast road (A55) from Bangor to Conwy.
LENGTH
30½ miles (49 km)
ASCENT
13,000 ft (3950 m)

There are fourteen summits over 3000 ft (914 m) in the Snowdonia National Park: three on Snowdon, five in the Glyder-Elidir Fawr Group and the remaining six in the Carneddau. To reach all of these summits in a single walk is a formidable undertaking that has long been recognized as a test of walking ability; as with the last walk, it is a task only for the very few. Traditionally, the summit of Snowdon is the starting point, which can legitimately be reached by the mountain railway, and that of Foel-fras the finishing point. This route has been chosen, like the last one, for its superb qualities as a walk, not for its potential as a race track.

Route Description

Follow Route 27 along the Watkin Path to the summit of Yr Wyddfa, along the arm of the Horseshoe to Crib-goch and down to Pen-y-Pass. In the road turn L and follow it for 3½ miles (5.5 km) through the Pass of Llanberis to Nant Peris.

Turn R along a side road just before the Pehoboth Chapel and follow this road as far as a gate by a cottage. Go through the gate and along the farm road beyond; roughly half-way to the next gate turn R on a path and go up the field to the L of barns to a ladder stile. Continue to a gate and then bend L with the wall along a farm road. After a few yards, turn R up the hill to reach a higher farm road, there turn L. Follow this farm road to a bridge over the stream to the L (by some quarry heaps). Cross the bridge and immediately turn R to follow the stream to a ladder stile over a fence. After the stile, strike half L up a very long slope (i.e. approximately due north) over grass and then boulders to eventually reach the summit of Elidir Fawr.

From the summit descend approximately due east along the ridge to pick up a path. This path descends (there is a cliff to the L) and then goes in a great curve across the hillside to the R. Keep along the ridge beyond, crossing the summits of Foel-goch

The old tramway from the South Snowdon Slate Quarry crossed by the Watkin Path

and Y Garn, to descend later to a small lake, Llyn y Cŵn. (Fences have been erected to the west of Foel-goch, and between Y Garn and Llyn y Cŵn which should be crossed at stiles.) Pass the lake on its L shore and pick up a path which climbs the slope ahead (this is very well cairned in its upper reaches). Follow this up to the summit of Glyder Fawr (the path bends to the L near to the summit). Continue along the ridge from the summit to reach spires of rock (The Castle of the Winds), which should be passed on the R side, and then the summit of Glyder Fach.

Beyond the summit, pass the Cantilever (a large horizontal projecting slab of rock) and on to the top of Bristly Ridge. Descend down scree to the R of Bristly Ridge to reach a col. Cross the wall there at a ladder stile and continue with the wall to the R. Keep in roughly the same direction up the South Ridge of Tryfan, carefully choosing your own path through the small crags and boulders to eventually reach the summit. Continue over the summit in approximately the same direction, choosing your route with great care, to descend the North Ridge (it will probably be much easier if you have already ascended this from Ogwen on a previous occasion). At a shoulder much lower down, descend to the L to a wall; there turn R and follow a path down to the Bangor-Capel Curig road (A5). Turn L and walk to Ogwen.

Follow Route 27 from Ogwen to Aber on the North Wales coast traversing the great ridge of the Carneddau.

The first section of the route over Snowdon can be varied in a number of ways, which include:

a) Instead of descending to Pen-y-Pass from the summit of Crib-goch, a descent can be made down the thin and steep ridge to the north of the summit. If carefully followed, avoiding crags, this leads to the road nearer to Nant Peris than Pen-y-Pass, thus avoiding some of the road walking.
b) An alternative start can be made from Pen-y-Pass over Crib-goch and Crib-y-ddysgl and using the Llanberis Path for the descent. This can be followed to Llanberis for a return along the road to Nant Peris.

As with Route 27, the walk can be completed over three days, staying overnight in the Llanberis and Ogwen valleys. In this case the three sections will involve:

Bethania to Pen-y-Pass 7 miles (11 km) 3860 ft (1170 m)
Pen-y-Pass to Ogwen 12½ miles (20 km) 5500 ft (1670 m)
Ogwen to Aber 11 miles (17.5 km) 3650 ft (1110 m)

The Watkin Path by the Gladstone Rock

Appendices

Access for the Walker

It is important to realize at the outset that the designation of a National Park does not change the ownership of the land within it in any way. In the case of the Snowdonia National Park, for example, in 1980, over thirty years after designation, only 0.3% of the land area was actually owned by the Park Authority, and only 30.5% by all 'public' bodies combined, e.g., National Trust, Ministry of Defence, etc. The laws of access and trespass apply just as much to areas of private land within a National Park as to those outside it.

The National Parks and Access to the Countryside Act of 1949 required County Councils in England and Wales to prepare maps which showed all paths over which the public had a right to walk. The final form of the map is referred to as a definitive map and copies are held at the offices of the County Council and District Council and sometimes by the Community Council concerned. The inclusion of a public right-of-way on a definitive map can be taken as proof that such exists. Paths can only be diverted or deleted from a definitive map by the raising of a Diversion Order or an Extinguishment Order respectively. The paths are classified as either footpaths (for walkers only) or bridleways (for walkers, horseriders and cyclists). Those public rights-of-way were included on the now withdrawn 1 inch to 1 mile (1:63 360) Seventh Series, the 1:25 000 Second Series (i.e. Pathfinder), 1:50 000 First and Second Series (i.e. Landranger) and the Outdoor Leisure maps.

It is obvious, however, that if this was the end of the matter, the right of access for the walker within the Snowdonia National Park would be severely restricted. There are considerable areas of land without any public rights-of-way and they do in fact reach only three mountain summits — Yr Wyddfa, Foel grach (almost) and Penygadair. Furthermore, in many cases, public rights-of-way terminate abruptly in strange out-of-the-way spots; this arose, for example, across a boundary where the owners or councils on opposite sides took different views over the existence of a right of way.

Fortunately, however, access to large areas is allowed in practice under one or more of the following:

NATIONAL TRUST AREAS

In 1980 the National Trust owned 8.8%, 43,533 acres (18,265 hectares) of the area of the Park. The Trust policy is to give free access at all times to its open spaces; however, there cannot, of course, be unrestricted access to tenanted farms, young plantations and woods, or certain nature reserves where the preservation of rare fauna and flora is paramount.

FORESTRY COMMISSION FORESTS

Particularly within the Beddgelert, Coed-y-Brenin, Dyfi, Gwydyr and Penllyn forests where walkers are allowed to walk along any paths or forest roads provided, of course, that they behave in a safe and sensible manner.

COURTESY FOOTPATHS

A number of footpaths have, with the landowners' agreement, been opened for public use although not in themselves being legal rights-of-way. The Miners' Track from near the Pen-y-Gwryd Hotel to Ogwen Cottage and the Precipice Walk are in this category. A Courtesy Footpath to the summit ridge of the Aran Mountains has been created recently. This runs approximately due south from Llanuwchllyn over Aran Benllyn and Aran Fawddwy to link up with public rights-of-way.

The agreement for the use of this path is reviewed annually.

ACCESS AGREEMENTS
Under the National Parks and Access to the Countryside Act of 1949, National Park Authorities have the power to negotiate Access Agreements with landowners whereby access is given in return for compensation in the form of a grant. This access may be subject to conditions as appropriate to the area.

Up to end 1985 twenty Access Agreements had been concluded in the Snowdonia National Park.

TRADITION
Walkers have for very many years walked freely in some of the hill and mountain areas of the Park with the tacit agreement of the landowners concerned, even though they may have had no legal right to do so. The tolerance shown will vary from farmer to farmer and, in any case, depends for its continuation upon the sensible behaviour of the walkers themselves. Litter, broken glass, ruined walls, unruly dogs, noisy behaviour, etc., are likely to make it more difficult for the next people to go that way.

It must be emphasized that on some of the walks described in this guide there are stretches where there is no legal right of way for the general public, and the walks are described on that understanding — see page 24. The local attitude to access may also obviously change with time.

Safety

The routes described in this guide vary considerably in both length and difficulty. Some at least of the easy walks should with reasonable care be safe at any time of the year and under almost any weather conditions; the more difficult walks on the other hand cross some of the wildest and roughest country in Great Britain and should only be attempted by fit walkers who are properly clothed and equipped and have command of the techniques involved in walking, scrambling and route finding.

It cannot be too strongly emphasized that weather and conditions can change very rapidly in mountain areas, during a day, from one part of a mountain to another or as you climb to higher ground. This must be borne in mind when selecting clothing and equipment before a walk. The severity of a walk will also generally be much greater in the winter when snow and ice are lying on the mountain than in the summer months. A route such as the Snowdon Horseshoe, for example, which should be within the reach of any reasonably fit and competent group in summer can become a difficult undertaking even for experienced mountaineers in the depth of winter.

The golden rules for safety in mountain and moorland areas are:

DO
Carry appropriate clothing and equipment, all of which should be in sound condition.
Carry map and compass and be practised in their use.
Leave a note of your intended route with a responsible person (and keep to it!).
Report your return as soon as possible.
Keep warm, but not overwarm, at all times.
Eat nourishing foods and rest at regular intervals.
Avoid becoming exhausted.
Know First Aid and the correct procedure in case of accidents or illness.
Obtain a weather forecast before you start. A

weather forecast with a report on ground conditions may be obtained all the year round from Llanberis (0286) 870120. Information boards around Snowdon give this information on winter weekends and in the peak summer season.

DO NOT
Go out on your own unless you are very experienced; three is a good number.
Leave any member of the party behind on the mountain, unless help has to be summoned.
Explore old mine workings, quarries or caves, or climb cliffs (except scrambling ridges).
Attempt routes which are beyond your skill and experience.

A booklet, *Safety on Mountains,* is published by the British Mountaineering Council, Crawford House, Precinct Centre, Booth Street East, Manchester, M13 9RZ.

Giving a Grid Reference

Giving a grid reference is an excellent way of 'pin-pointing' a feature, such as a church or mountain summit, on an Ordnance Survey map.

Grid lines, which are used for this purpose, are shown on the 1:25 000 Outdoor Leisure, 1:25 000 Pathfinder and 1:50 000 Landranger maps produced by the Ordnance Survey; these are the maps most commonly used by walkers. They are the thin blue lines (one kilometre apart) going vertically and horizontally across the map producing a network of small squares. Each line, whether vertical or horizontal, is given a number from 00 to 99, with the sequence repeating itself every 100 lines. The 00 lines are slightly thicker than the others thus producing large squares with sides made up of 100 small squares and thus representing 100 kilometres. Each of these large squares is identified by two letters. The entire network of lines covering the British Isles, excluding Ireland, is called the National Grid.

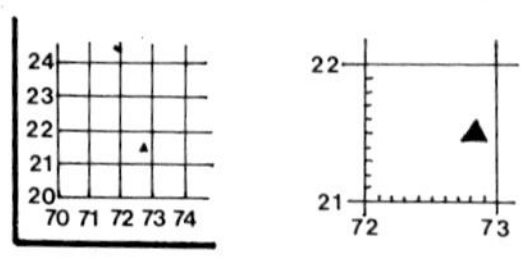

FIGURE 3 Giving a grid reference

This shows a corner of an Ordnance Survey 1:50 000 Landranger map which contains a Youth Hostel. Using this map, the method of determining a grid reference is as follows:

Step 1
Holding the map in the normal upright position, note the number of the 'vertical' grid line to the left of the hostel. This is 72.
Step 2
Now imagine that the space between this grid line and the adjacent one to the right of the hostel is divided into ten equal divisions (the diagram on the right does this for you). Estimate the number of these 'tenths' that the hostel lies to the right of the left-hand grid line. This is 8. Add this to the number found in Step 1 to make 728.
Step 3
Note the number of the grid line below the hostel and add it on to the number obtained above. This is 21, so that the number becomes 72821.
Step 4
Repeat Step 2 for the space containing the hostel, but now in a vertical direction. The final number to be added is 5, making 728215. This is called a six-figure grid reference. This, coupled with the number or name of the appropriate Landranger or Outdoor Leisure map, will enable the Youth Hostel to be found.

A full grid reference will also include the identification of the appropriate 100 kilometre square of the National Grid; for example, SD 728215. This information is given in the margin of each map.

Countryside Access Charter

YOUR RIGHTS OF WAY ARE

Public footpaths — on foot only Sometimes waymarked in yellow

Bridleways — on foot, horseback and pedal cycle Sometimes waymarked in blue

Byways (usually old roads), most 'Roads Used as Public Paths' and, of course, public roads — all traffic

Use maps, signs and waymarks. Ordnance Survey Pathfinder and Landranger maps show most public rights of way

ON RIGHTS OF WAY YOU CAN

Take a pram, pushchair or wheelchair if practicable

Take a dog (on a lead or under close control)

Take a short route round an illegal obstruction or remove it sufficiently to get past

YOU HAVE A RIGHT TO GO FOR RECREATION TO

Public parks and open spaces — on foot

Most commons near older towns and cities — on foot and sometimes on horseback

Private land where the owner has a formal agreement with the local authority

IN ADDITION YOU CAN USE BY LOCAL OR ESTABLISHED CUSTOM OR CONSENT, BUT ASK FOR ADVICE IF YOU'RE UNSURE

Many areas of open country like moorland, fell and coastal areas, especially those of the National Trust, and some commons

Some woods and forests, especially those owned by the Forestry Commission

Country Parks and picnic sites

Most beaches

Canal towpaths

Some private paths and tracks. Consent sometimes extends to riding horses and pedal cycles

FOR YOUR INFORMATION

County councils and London boroughs maintain and record rights of way, and register commons

Obstructions, dangerous animals, harassment and misleading signs on rights of way are illegal and you should report them to the county council

Paths across fields can be ploughed, but must normally be reinstated within two weeks

Landowners can require you to leave land to which you have no right of access

Motor vehicles are normally permitted only on roads, byways and some 'Roads Used as Public Paths'

Follow any local by-laws

AND, WHEREVER YOU GO, FOLLOW THE COUNTRY CODE

Enjoy the countryside and respect its life and work

Guard against all risk of fire

Fasten all gates

Keep your dogs under close control

Keep to public paths across farmland

Use gates and stiles to cross fences, hedges and walls

Leave livestock, crops and machinery alone

Take your litter home

Help to keep all water clean

Protect wildlife, plants and trees

Take special care on country roads

Make no unnecessary noise

This Charter is for practical guidance in England and Wales only. It was prepared by the Countryside Commission.

Addresses of Useful Organizations

British Trust for Conservation Volunteers,
36 St Mary's Street,
Wallingford,
Oxfordshire, OX10 0EU.
Wallingford (0491) 39766
(Regional Office:
Conservation Volunteers,
The Wales Conservation Centre,
Forest Farm,
Forest Farm Road,
Whitchurch,
Cardiff, CF4 7JH.
Cardiff (0222) 626660)
For those who wish to help with countryside conservation, e.g. repairing drystone walls, maintaining footpaths, at weekends or holiday times.

The Camping and Caravaning Club,
11 Lower Grosvenor Place,
London, SW1W 0EY.
01-828 1012

Council for National Parks,
45 Shelton Street,
London, WC2H 9HJ.
01-235 0901

Countryside Commission,
John Dower House,
Crescent Place,
Cheltenham,
Gloucestershire, GL50 3RA.
Cheltenham (0242) 521381

Countrywide Holidays Association,
323 Birch Heys,
Cromwell Range,
Manchester, M14 6HU.
061-225 1000

Forestry Commission,
Victoria House,
Victoria Terrace,
Aberystwyth,
Dyfed, SY23 2DG.
Aberystwyth (0970) 612367
All publications on forestry and the work of the Commission.

HF Holidays Ltd.,
142–144 Great North Way,
Hendon,
London, NW4 1EG.
01-203 3381

The Long Distance Walkers Association,
Membership Secretary,
Kevin Uzzell,
7 Forest Drive,
Yarnfield,
Stone,
Staffordshire, ST15 0RP.
Stafford (0785) 760684

The National Trust,
36 Queen Anne's Gate,
London, SW1H 9AS.
01-222 9251
(Regional Office for North Wales:
Trinity Square,
Llandudno,
Gwynedd, LL30 2DE.
Llandudno (0492) 860123)

Nature Conservancy Council,
North Wales Region,
Plas Penrhos,
Fford Penrhos,
Bangor,
Gwynedd, LL57 2LQ.
Bangor (0248) 370444
For permits to enter reserves and for publications.

Ramblers' Association,
1/5 Wandsworth Road,
London, SW8 2XX.
01-582 6878

Snowdonia National Park,
Penrhyndeudraeth,
Gwynedd, LL48 6LS.
Penrhyndeudraeth (0766) 770274
For all Snowdonia National Park Committee publications.

The Snowdonia National Park Society,
(Cymdeithas Parc Cenedlaethol Eryri),
The Ugly House,
Capel Curig,
Near Betws-y-Coed,
Gwynedd.
Capel Curig (069 04) 234
Founded in 1968, dedicated to serving the National Park and preserving its charm and character.

Wales Tourist Board,
Brunel House,
2 Fitzalan Road,
Cardiff, CF2 1UY.
Cardiff (0222) 499909
General publications for the whole of Wales.

Youth Hostels Association (England and Wales),
Trevelyan House,
8 St Stephen's Hill,
St Albans,
Hertfordshire, AL1 2DY.
St Albans (0727) 55215

Index

Place names and sites of interest only are included. Page numbers in *italics* refer to illustrations.

Aber 38, 172
Aber Falls, 38, *39*, 40
Aberglaslyn Pass 49, *51*, 54, 114
Afon Clywedog 28, *29*, *31*
Afon Conwy 42
Afon Llugwy *31*, *33*, 88
Afon Mawddach 34, 35

Beddgelert 49, 56, 75, 114
  Forest 78
Bethania 120, 178, 182, 184
Bethesda 20, 21
Betws-y-Coed 32, 42
Blaenau Ffestiniog 20, 21
Bontnewydd 38, *41*, 172
Bristly Ridge 168–170, *169*, 183
Britannia Copper Mine 126, 167
Bwlch Tyddiad 46, *47*, 71
Bwlch y Moch 159
Bwlch y Sygyn 49

Cader Idris 68, *69*, 95–8, *97*, *99*
Cantilever 82
Capel Curig 88, 100
Carnedd Dafydd 157, 158
Carnedd Llewelyn 149–158, 172
Carneddau 100–106, 149, 172–7, *175*
  Welsh 1000 Metres 178
  Welsh Three Thousands 182
Carneddi 119
Castell Caer Lleion 66
Cnicht 114–9
Coedydd Aber Nature Trail 40
Coed y Brenin Forest 34, 35, 36
Conwy 62
  Castle 66
  Mountain 62–6
Craig yr Ysfa 156
Crib-goch 159, 160, *161*
Cwm Bychan 46, 49–56, 71
Cwm Dyli 128, 159, 163
Cwm Idwal 57–60

Devil's Kitchen 57, 58, 80, 81, 85
Dinas Emrys 52
Dinorwic Quarry 21, 146, 148
Dolgellau 28, 34, 35, 68
Dorothea Quarry 21
Dyffryn Mymbyr 84

Eigiau Dam 176
Elidir Fawr 142–8

Foel Cynwch 34, 35
Foel Faner 34, 35
Foel grach Refuge 176–7

Gladstone Rock 120, 126
Glasdir arboretum 36
Gloyw Lyn 71, 72
Glyder
  Fach 80, 82, 168, 183
  Fawr 80, *85*, 180
  Ridge 80–6, *87*
Gorphwysfa Hotel 163
Gorsedd stone circle 43, 45
Gwydyr Forest 30, 42–5

Hafod y Llan Quarry 126
Helyg 156

Idwal
  Skyline 168–170
  Slabs 58

Llanbedr 71
Llanberis 20, 145, 182
Llanrwst 42, 43, 45
Llugwy Gorge 30–2
Llydaw Causeway 128
Llyn
  Cowlyd 100, *105*, 106
  Crafnant 100, 106, *107*
  Cynwch 34, 35
  Idwal 60
  Llagi 114
  Ogwen 60, *153*
  Parc 43
  y Cŵn 142–3
  yr Adar 114, 116

Maes y Gaer 40
Maes-y-garnedd 108, 112
Maesgwm Visitor Centre 36
Marchlyn Mawr 145
Mawddach 35
Miners'
  Bridge 32
  Track *87*, 120, 121, 167
Moel Hebog 75–8, *79*
Moel Siabod 88–94
Moel yr Ogof 78

Nant Ffrancon 60, *61*, 142–8
Nant Gwynant 52, 114
Nant Peris 142, 182
Nantlle Ridge 129–134
Nantmor 49, 52
Nebo 130

Oakwood Park 66
Ogof Owain Glyndŵr 78

Ogwen 57, 80, 149, 168, 172, 178
  Falls 60, 86, 155
  Valley 22, 149, *171*, 172

Parc Cenedlaethol Eryri 9–22, *24*
Pen-y-Gwryd 84–5
Pen-y-Pass 159, 178, 184
Penrhyn Quarry 21
Penygadair 68, *70*
Penyrole-wen 150–2, 172, *181*
Pig Track 159, 164
Plas y Brenin 88
Pont Aber Glaslyn 49, 50, 54
Pont-Scethin 140, *141*
Pont-y-Pair Bridge 30, 32, 42
Precipice Walk 34–6, *37*
Pyg Track *see* Pig Track

Rhaeadr-fawr 38, 40
Rhinog
  Fach 108, 109
  Fawr 71–4, 108, *110–111*
  National Nature Reserve 48
Rhinogydd 22, 108–112, 135–140
Roman Steps 46–8, *47*, 71
Ryd-ddu 129

Snowdon 120–8, 178, 182
  Horseshoe *89*, 120, *127*, 159–167
  Mountain Railway 164, 166
Snowdonia
  Forest Park 14
  National Park 9–22, *24*
Stephenson's Tubular Bridge 66
Swallow Falls 30, 32
Sychnant Pass 62–6, *65*

Taly-y-bont 135
Telford's
  Suspension Bridge *63*, 66
  Turnpike 155
Torrent Walk 28
Trawsfynydd 138–40
Tryfan 168–170, *169*, *171*
Tu-hwnt-i'r-bont 45
Ty-hyll *see* Ugly House

Ugly House 30, 31–2

Wangeheng 52
Watkin Path 120, 122, 126
Welsh Highland Railway 49, 54–5, 75, 134

Y Garn 129, 142–8, *147*
Y Llethr 135, 136
Y Lliwedd 159, 162–3, 167
Yr Wyddfa *123*, 124, 126, 159